VESTMENTS
FOR ALL SEASONS

VESTMENTS
FOR ALL SEASONS

BARBARA DEE BAUMGARTEN

MOREHOUSE PUBLISHING
A Continuum imprint
HARRISBURG • LONDON • NEW YORK

For St. Clare of Assisi,
my brothers and sisters of the
Society of St. Francis, Third Order,
and for the women at the
Drucilla Balaba Training School,
Kabale, Uganda

Copyright © 2002 by Barbara Dee Baumgarten

Morehouse Publishing
A Continuum Imprint
P.O. Box 321
Harrisburg, PA 17105

Unless otherwise noted, the Scripture quotations are from the *New Revised Standard Version Bible*, copyright © 1989 by the Division of Christian Education of the National Council of the Churches of Christ in the U.S.A. Used by permission. All rights reserved.

The Scripture quotation from the *New King James Version* (NKJV), copyright © 1979, 1980, and 1982 by Thomas Nelson Publishers, Inc., Nashville, Tennessee.

The drawing at the beginning of chapter 1 is based on an excellent sketch of the early Christian chasuble by Anastasia Dolby in her book *Church Vestments, Their Origin, Use and Ornament*, copyright © 1868 by Chapman and Hall Publishers, London, England.

Design by Corey Kent
Photography by Karen Weyer

Baumgarten, Barbara Dee Bennett, 1955–
   Vestments for all seasons / Barbara Dee Baumgarten.
      p. cm.
Includes bibliographical references (p.   ) and index.
   ISBN 0-8192-1866-9
   1. Church vestments. I. Title.
   BV167 .B38 2002
   247—dc21

                          2002006722

Printed in the United States of America
02 03 04 05 06   6 5 4 3 2 1

CONTENTS

$\backsim$

PART II: THE PATTERNS

PREFACE

〜

How can [I] thank God enough for you in return for all the joy that [I] feel before God because of you?

—1 Thessalonians 3:9

Deep in history, the church fathers wore simple, flowing garments that reflected the style of their day. Over 2,000 years later, church vestments have retained their classic shapes, but they can be far more lavish. Frequently they are embellished with elaborate appliqué, embroidery, and quilting. Because they are often so ornately adorned, and so steeped in the symbolism and history of the church, vestments have acquired a mystique. Even those who sew well can feel too intimidated to make them. But the joy and satisfaction of creating vestments need not be limited to an elite few. Vestments, like other elements of worship, are best when they are made as gifts by the people of God.

To encourage the art of vestment making, this book covers the history, unique qualities, and spirituality associated with these liturgical garments and altar cloths, as well as elements of design. A glossary of church attire in the second chapter lists various vestments and their uses. The book includes patterns and methods for making vestments, as well as tips on contemporary methods for traditional adornment: appliqué, painting, and piecing. I hope these instructions reduce the fear factor and stimulate the hearts and imaginations of all those attracted to vestment design and construction.

Making a vestment involves two steps: adorning or preparing the fabric, then constructing the garment. The patterns in this book are for those with a novice-to-intermediate skill level. The garment construction is uncomplicated; the challenge lies in the adornment. What most of the projects require is persistence. Vestment making is not difficult, but it does require

many steps to complete. To ensure that your projects are a success, allow plenty of time to follow the basic steps. Most of the projects lend themselves well to a group effort, making "little work for many hands."

NOTES ON USING THIS BOOK

Fabric requirements and particular notions are found at the beginning of each chapter. Staple notions are listed at the beginning of chapter 5.

All illustrations are numbered according to chapter number and the order they appear within the chapter. For example, Figure 1-1 is the first illustration in chapter 1. Beginning with chapter 5, a letter and number are added to the chapter number. The letter tells you which vestment you are working on (see the codes below); the number following it indicates the step in the construction process. For example, Figure 5-BS2 is the illustration for the second step for making a bias strip found in chapter 5. The letters used include (in alphabetical order):

BS – Bias Strips
 B – Binding in chapter 5; Burse thereafter
 C – Cording in chapter 5, Chasuble thereafter
DT – Dalmatic/Tunicle
 D – Deacon's stole
 M – Maniple
 P – Paraments
PS – Pocket Stole
 S – Stole
 V – Chalice Veil

I am indebted and grateful to the church for its endurance, its encouragement, and its creativity through the years; to St. Clare of Assisi, who profoundly understood the bond between prayer and handwork; to Phyllis Stevens, who provided the pattern for a cowled chasuble and taught me how to make it; to Ed Miller and Ann Graham, who contributed fabric woven by the late Virginia Miller, an expert weaver; to the Reverend Gale Morris, who made the Easter rainbow chasuble; to Leslie Carson, who led the Sunday school that made the Easter stole; to Pattiann Bennett, Clara Hazelwood, and Cynthia Davis, whose insightful and adept reading of my manuscript was indispensable; to my editor at Morehouse Publishing, Debra Farrington, whose support and patience sustained the writing of this book; to Nancy Fitzgerald and Christine Finnegan for their expert supervision of the text and multiple illustrations; to Corey Kent, for the lovely book design; to my photographer, Karen Weyer, and her assistant, Hector Arbour, for their fine skill and flexibility; to Ronda Scullen, typesetter extraordinaire; and to my family, whose love and humor endure the vicissitudes of living with a writer-artist.

PART I
PREPARATION

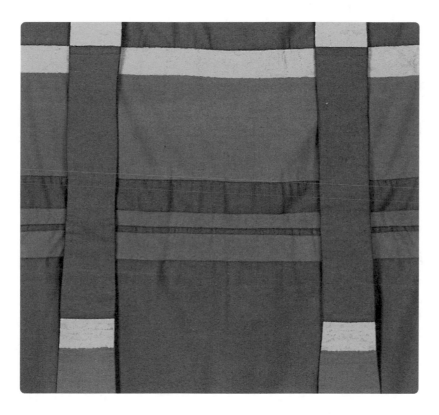

1.
SEEKING UNIFORMITY AND DISTINCTION: A HISTORICAL OVERVIEW

❦

*The necessities of life are water, bread and clothing,
and also a house to assure privacy.*

—Sirach 29:21

Shelter, food, and clothing are the necessities of human life. The Christian Eucharistic celebration incorporates and sanctifies these essentials as a sign to us that life in Christ is not peripheral to daily life but basic to it. Christians gather in a shelter designated sacred to share a simple meal of bread and wine. The ministers of the meal don particular garments, special to the occasion. While Jesus himself determined the food for the liturgical rite—and the shelter or church was instituted quickly thereafter—the idea of special liturgical clothing came much later. The garments designated for the ceremonies of the church are called "vestments." Ministers wear them to celebrate the Eucharist and other sacramental rites, for the Offices of prayer, and for other public services.

Even in the earliest books of the Bible, God directed that his ministers wear specific apparel. God commanded Moses to remove his shoes while on the mountain (Exodus 3:5) and directed that Moses' brother Aaron wear special clothing to set him apart as a priest: "You shall make sacred vestments for the glorious adornment of your brother Aaron. And you shall speak to all who have ability, whom I have endowed with skill, that they make Aaron's vestments to consecrate him for my priesthood" (Exodus 28:2–4; compare Exodus 20:26; 29:4–9; 28:42; 39:27–28, and Leviticus 16:3–4).

While the Hebrew Scriptures show concern for the dress of their ministers, the New Testament is quiet on the subject. The few references to clothing relate to garments worn by people other than ministers. In one account, Paul instructs women to wear a head covering while praying or prophesying (1 Corinthians 11:5); John of Patmos describes the white garments of the saints (Revelation 19:6–9); and Paul asks Timothy to bring him his cloak when they meet (2 Timothy 4:13). If Paul's cloak had any liturgical significance, it would have been a garment to remove for prayer (a heathen custom), not one to put on. The New Testament's silence makes it hardly surprising that the Jesus movement and the early church did not use prescribed garb for ministers at the Eucharist.

The ancient church had little fear of adapting and adopting common practices. In his life and preaching, Jesus turned ideas of purity and separation upside down. Therefore, his earliest followers found insufficient cause to be different or separate from the common folk. They aspired to be *in* the world without being *of* the world. Wearing the common dress displayed solidarity with the people (in the world) while distinctive dress would have emphasized separation or fashion-consciousness (of the world).

Jesus, the new king, advocated affiliation with the poor and resisted separation from people with different beliefs and lifestyles. After Jesus' death, when the church was new, floundering, and under persecution, the ministers were more than affiliated with the poor: they were poor themselves. They could hardly afford extra or special clothing for their Eucharistic gatherings. Moreover, wearing the common dress of the Roman peasant avoided distinguishing trappings that may have triggered persecution. Out of a need for protective homogeneity, poor status, and a reconciling adaptability, the roots of the new Christian church—its liturgy, holy days, buildings, and vestments—were rooted in the domestic and civil realm of ancient Rome.

The Levitical or Jewish temple priests' dress code is the first one we know of describing prescribed dress for a particular group. They wore white/natural linen breeches, a tunic, girdle, and bonnet. For sanctuary service they added "golden vestments" woven with threads of gold, purple, blue, and scarlet, including a dark blue robe (*meïl*); a breastplate, (*choshen*); a front-let (*ephod*); and a gold head-plate (*tzitz*). Perhaps some of the apostles adopted components of the Jewish priestly dress as a way to designate their corresponding role in the new Jesus sect. By tradition, James wore linen and a golden plate upon his head and John wore the golden breastplate.[1] Yet no correlation exists between the Levitical vestments and the ensuing Christian vestments.

Wearing uniforms is a basic human tendency. Besides identifying a person's function and office, they also herald ceremonial occasions. They are usually worn within a particular domain (a church or hospital, for example) and often signify that domain's hierarchy (priest, deacon, acolyte, or doctor, nurse, volunteer). They may also demonstrate a complexity of interrelations by using color, shape, design, and insignia that provide clues to rank and relationship to others, as we see in military uniforms.

Because those who wear them are not expressing their own style, uniforms signify more about the group or organization to which those persons belong than the personality of the wearers. When ministers don their clerical garb, the worshiping community is not distracted by the poverty or wealth, the trendy or conventional dress of a particular minister. Rather, the attention of the congregation is diverted away from the wearer—and away from any fashionable affiliations his or her street clothing may represent—to the collective authority and meaning of the church that the vestments represent.

Normally, clothes provide information about the wearer and elicit a response from those who see them. We pay close attention to what we wear to a job interview or on a first date, because we know that our clothing makes an immediate and influential impression. We wear particular clothes for specific activities: a swimsuit at the pool; a business suit at the office; a new outfit for a twenty-fifth wedding anniversary. In each case, the clothing signals something about the activity taking place and why folks have gathered. A member of the clergy, for instance, is often referred to as "a person of the cloth." (This phrase may refer to the medieval practice of the clergy to wrap their necks with cloth to protect their throats and voices from the cold.) Vestments, which are essentially in-house uniforms worn over public uniforms, remind congregations why they are gathered. Ultimately, vestments silently point the congregation's attention to God, the reason for worship and the heart of it.

The vestments of the Christian church derive from both the common and imperial attire of ancient Rome, and have been regulated over the years by custom and rule. The use of distinctive clothing first began around the time of Constantine (circa 274–337) when the ministers of the church began to adopt the respectable clothes specific to state and solemn occasions. And it is these clothes, the fashions of imperial Rome, that provide the basic template of the vestments we know and use today. Over the years these fashions have not changed, largely because of the clergy's conservative attitude toward the fickle fashions of the world. The church continues to cherish tradition in order to maintain continuity with Jesus and the ancient church. Yet periods of modification have alternated with periods of consistent style. There are three distinctive periods in the development of vestments: the first through eighth centuries—the period of origin and definition; the ninth through eighteenth centuries—the era of change and opulence; the nineteenth century through modern times—the time of simplification and revival.

Vestments began as the ordinary clothing of ordinary folk. As secular styles changed, the clergy resisted worldly influences, and eventually these older styles were retained only by the church, which determined uses and wearers. At first vestments were utilitarian, completely lacking in symbolism. The clothing and vessels of the first-century church were the everyday wares of domestic life. The ordinary drinking cup and plate served as the chalice and paten, and the longer common tunic served as a sign of civility, because barbarians wore short garments. Even the partially shaved head, called a "tonsure" in later centuries, began as a common Roman hairstyle, which differentiated them from barbarians, who wore their hair long.

The ordinary dress of a first-century priest was the dress of the poor. It consisted of a simple tunic of varying length that was sometimes sleeved. As the role of the bishop began to take on definition, the bishop's hemline lengthened to signal authority. Since persecution prevented early Christian leaders from wearing overtly prescribed dress, length served as a subtle clue to clerical authority. Another garment that could be worn safely was the *pallium*, a large, rectangular, outdoor garment that when worn alone designated a

Figure 1-1. The pallium.

Figure 1-2. The byrrus.

Figure 1-3. The open-front
paenula.

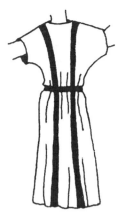

Figure 1-4. The tunica
with clavi.

"man of thought"—a philosopher or a student (Figure 1-1). Later, the *pallium* was deemed the traditional mantle of Christ. Possible upper-body garments included a cowled, woolen cape called a *byrrus* or *birrus* (Figure 1-2) or a rough, hooded cloak called a *paenula* (Figure 1-3). For the most part, however, the early church resisted uniformed clerics. Early writings and mandates from the councils consistently encouraged the clergy to dress with commonality and moderation, not for show, "as if there were some holiness in that" (Council of Gangra, circa 345).[2]

As the church and its hierarchy became more established, the tendency to make distinct garments for the ministers grew. With support from the local congregation, the once too-poor presbyter could afford proper "Sunday" clothing, usually the clothing of the Roman gentry, which was preferred for special occasions.

A Roman citizen wore a tunic, a wide, shirt-like undergarment, girded to a length denoting rank and gender. Originally sleeveless and later sleeved and light-colored, it was adorned with two purple vertical running stripes (*clavi*), which varied in width according to the status of the wearer. A lesser person wore narrow stripes; a person of greater eminence wore wide stripes. Senators wore a single wide stripe, or *clavus*. The early Christians favored a white linen tunic with two ordinary *clavi* (Figure 1-4).

The Roman citizen's toga, a single broad, semicircular piece of cloth worn loosely over the tunic, began as a garment of the Roman lower classes. They eventually abandoned it, because it was too cumbersome for daily toil and travel. Rome's male citizens adopted the impractical toga as their garment of peace, wearing it over the *tunica* for solemn occasions or for public appearances as a symbol of status (Figure 1-5). The early Christians followed suit and adopted the toga

over the tunic for worship. The clothing choice served to highlight the importance of worship and the presbyter's prominence within the Christian movement, while simultaneously avoiding a distinctive dress that might arouse suspicion leading to persecution.

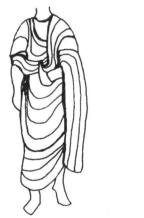

Figure 1-5. Roman toga.

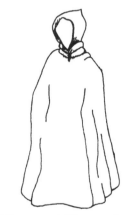

Figure 1-6. The casula *or
closed-front* paenula.

The *paenula* or *casula* (Figure 1-6), another garment of the poor, eventually replaced the toga. The *paenula* may be the most common and universal of human protective attire worn throughout the ages. In modern America we call it a poncho. It consists of a large piece of cloth with a hole cut in the middle for the head to pass through. Usually a hood is attached to the cloth. In ancient Rome, the poor regularly wore a dark coarse fabric or leather *paenula*, while the upper classes assumed it solely for travel in foul weather. However, during the fourth century, the *paenula* gained a place of dignity among the Roman upper classes, and those made from fine cloth became favored garments.

Concurrent with the *paenula*'s growth in popularity among the wealthy, the Edict of Milan, instituted by the Roman Emperor Constantine in 313 C.E., ended the persecution of the church. Civil toleration and status prompted Christians to continue wearing the *paenula*, now a label of distinction. Christianity's legalization freed Christian leaders to wear garments and accessories that openly reflected their positions within the church and simultaneously displayed their new-found status within Roman society. This, in turn, spurred Christian leaders to issue mandates to the clergy to avoid distinctive clothing. Except for the bishop, they were advised to dress the same way as the people. When Constantine united the Christian church to the civil order, the bishops acquired a status that warranted official dress; they wore the clothing of civil authority to signify their episcopal dignity. The clergy in general, however, dressed as they always had, in the garments of the common folk.

In 330, another hallmark of Constantine's rule was the relocation of the empire's capital to Byzantium, renamed Constantinople. A Christian city from its inception, Constantinople and its bishop of the "New Rome" struggled with Rome and her bishop for pre-eminence within Christendom. Gradually, the Eastern Orthodox and the Western Catholic churches became estranged, resulting in a schism around 1054. The empire's shift to Constantinople and the progressive separation between the more Greek and Oriental East and the classical and Roman West accounts for the distinctive vestments found within the two strains of the Christian church. Our focus is on the development of vestments in the Western church.

Around 400 C.E., the Teutons of Northern Europe began to push their way into Rome; then, in 476, the Vandals from Africa conquered Rome, bringing antiquity to a close. These uneducated warriors, commonly called barbarians by the educated and cultured Romans, thoroughly revolutionized Roman culture and brought with them a change in fashion. The barbarians brought into high fashion their short garments designed for the active life, the *cottus* and the *sagum*, a scant tunic and a rectangular cloak. Gone were the long, flowing civil garments of repose, except in the Christian church. Conservatives within the church resisted the fashion changes and for the first time the clergy became distinguished by their dress during worship. The flowing attire of the Roman gentleman became specifically liturgical, though their precisely sacerdotal and Eucharistic associations remained unapparent.

Change for the sake of change was not characteristic of the church; liturgical vestments continued to reflect their apostolic roots. During the fourth and fifth centuries, Christianity established itself as an institution distinct from the secular realm and maintained a style of dress similar to what Jesus and his followers wore. Church vestments now served as an outward expression of Christian identity, continuity, and endurance. Writings of the early church councils consistently opposed the new, short military *sagum* in favor of the conservative, long, and modest *paenula* or *casula*.

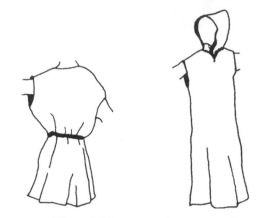

Figure 1-7. The colobium   *Figure 1-8. The* cuculla

The fall of Rome and the ensuing Middle Ages (476–1500) gave impetus to a fomenting movement within the church: monasticism. The monks adopted a homogeneous habit that consisted of a simple sleeveless tunic of rough linen, fashioned after the Roman *colobium* (Figure 1-7) a goatskin habit with a cowl derived from the *byrrus*, and a long black cloak adapted from the Roman hooded overgarment, the *cuculla* (Figure 1-8). In accordance with monastic vows of poverty and humility, the monk's habit mimicked the attire of the poor, whose clothing did not change with the caprice of fashion. The monk's habit, in turn, influenced the general dress of the clergy, particularly when a monk, Gregory the Great (590–604) was called to the chair of St. Peter. As Pope, Gregory organized many areas in the church, including the liturgy, the calendar, and clerical dress. Gregory opposed the new secular fashions and expected his clergy to follow suit with a version of the monk's long dark tunic and cowled cloak. His influence, like the council's, was not heeded in the secular realm. Clergy insisted on following the caprices of fashion, causing St. Boniface (675–754) a Benedictine monk, to decree a century later: "priests and deacons are not to use *saga* (short cloaks) like the laity, but *casulae*, like servants of God."[3]

Such disagreements have faced the church since the beginning. From the earliest days of the church, bishops and others met regularly to decide matters of the new faith. Their councils sought to codify essential doctrines, the orders of ministry, the calendar, the liturgy, and the vestments. But in spite of such efforts, vestments never achieved uniformity. Individual tastes as well as difference in the availability of materials and craftspeople accounted for variances, then as now. War, too, had an effect. Vestments were destroyed and were too costly to replace. A lack of uniformity has characterized vestment style and use throughout history.

Pope Gregory established a dress code for those who celebrated the Eucharist. He favored the simple, inexpensive, light linen tunic with scarlet *clavi*, a change from the earlier purple stripe. This band of fabric, with an occasional addition of fringe, was a status symbol corresponding to second-century Roman civil attire and evolved into the orphrey, or Y-shaped cross that still adorns vestments today. The use of a scarlet color as well as costly purple fabric accentuated the position of the clergy. As liturgical forms and Christian beliefs became standardized, so did vestments; the vestments we know today were in place by the ninth century. Once the garb of the clergy was determined, the constituent parts saw little change, yet their appearance changed a great deal through the years. How each piece developed is described in the following chapter. The general trend was from simple to progressively more ornate garments, and finally to excessively opulent attire, symbolizing the hierarchical corruption of the church. Eventually, these and other excesses in the church led to the Reformation, which began in the fourteenth century. Under the influence of the reformers, vestments were simplified for practicality.

During the Reformation many new attitudes emerged regarding vestments. Some Christians rejected the use of vestments altogether because they symbolized what was wrong with the church in general. The Reformed groups such as the Anabaptists, Zwinglians, and Calvinists held that the true ornaments of the minister were preaching the gospel and administering the sacraments. Vestments were not biblical, they maintained: they were papist, pompous, and distracting. Clergy were better off wearing the common lay dress or the sixteenth-century academic's black street gown. Other groups, less radical, rejected all vestments except the alb, since it did have biblical basis as the robe of Christ and the robe of the saints in Revelation. Its white simplicity did not lend itself to the elaborate ornamentation of other vestments, and it provided a uniform dress among the clergy. Martin Luther and his colleagues were indifferent toward vestments, believing they were insignificant. Clergy were free to continue wearing them or to discard them, as personal

preference and circumstances dictated. Finally, the more Catholic-oriented reformers favored vestments because they maintained unity and continuity with the ancient church. Vestments were not of theological import but they did play a positive role. They served as invitational windows to the holy; they inspired personal piety and differentiated the various ministers. After the Reformation, vestments or their absence became an outward sign of ecclesiastic theology, a denominational badge of sorts. The Calvinists, for example, rejected vestments along with the liturgical calendar and fixed liturgies. When the inclination to distinguish ministers did arise, the black Geneva gown was the sanctioned attire. Protestants who favored or were ambiguous about vestments never completely discontinued their use; the differing opinions created inconsistencies throughout post-Reformation denominations. Some Lutherans, for example, adopted the Geneva gown, while others maintained the alb, cincture, and chasuble. The Anglicans' vacillating and divergent use of vestments is representative of the more liturgically based Protestant denominations, especially when the denominations are considered worldwide. The first Book of Common Prayer of 1549 instructs Eucharistic ministers to wear a white alb with a vestment or cope. The vestment prescribed probably refers to the chasuble, although it may include the vestments for the priest, deacon, and subdeacon; that is, the chasuble, dalmatic, tunicle, the stoles of the first two orders, and the maniple worn by all three. The second Book of Common Prayer of 1552 forbade the wearing of the vestments promoted in the first prayer book. Retained were a surplice for the priest or a deacon and the rochet for the bishop. The Book of Common Prayer of 1559 simply states: "such ornaments of the church, and of the ministers thereof shall be retained, and be in use" without specifying which provisions in particular were being retained. This rubric, still in use today, has left interpretation wide open. From the introduction of the current Church of England Book of Common Prayer of 1662 until the Oxford movement (1833–1845) which sought to restore High Church ideals, the clergy favored the 1552 rubric. The Oxford movement prompted a revival of the 1549 Eucharistic vestments that remain in favor today.

In the American Book of Common Prayer of 1979 (BCP) there is no rubric specific to vestments, traditionally called an "ornaments rubric." The subject of vestments is addressed within the ordination rubrics. The BCP specifies that the ordinand wear a surplice or alb without other distinctive vesture and, after the prayer of consecration, directs the ordinand to be vested with the stole or other insignia appropriate to the particular order.[4] The bishop's rubric is even more vague: "and while the new bishop is being clothed with the vesture of the episcopate, instrumental music may be played."[5] Not even a stole is mentioned. These non-specific rubrics account for the great variety of vesture within the Anglican Communion. Some clergy don the full garb listed in the 1549 rubric; most advocate the traditional Eucharistic set minus the maniple, dalmatic, and tunicle; and others prefer a simple black cassock, surplice, and stole.

The Roman Catholic Church continues to follow the traditional complement of vestments set in the ninth century, with some variation since Vatican II. They consist of the inner garments—the amice and the alb girded with a cincture—and the outer garments, including the chasuble, dalmatic, and tunicle, and the insignia of rank, the maniple and stole. To these the bishop adds sandals, buskins, gloves, mitre, and insignia, including the ring and pectoral cross. When Vatican II (1963–1965) sought to simplify the liturgy and appropriate its particulars to the local community, they loosened the regulation of vestments as well. Many Roman Catholic and Anglican clergy abandoned the amice and maniple, the tunicle as well as the subdeacon's and often the deacon's dalmatic. These articles are retained in the American churches of today, primarily by the celebrants of the Anglican High Mass. Currently, a free-flowing alb worn with a pendant-style stole (the stole ends hang straight down the front) is gaining in popularity among clergy across denominational lines.

NOTES

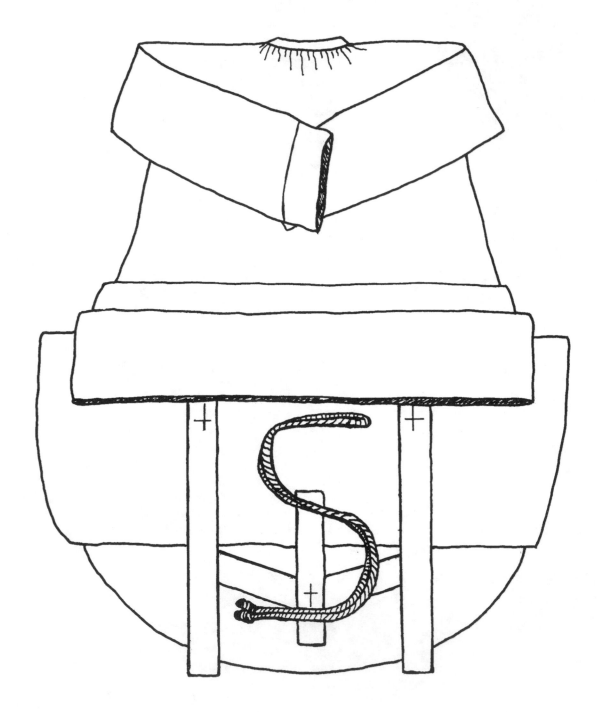

2.
IDENTIFYING THE PARTICULARS: A GLOSSARY

∾

*These are the vestments that they shall make: a breastpiece,
an ephod, a robe, a checkered tunic, a turban, and a sash.*

—Exodus 28:4

Vestments are grouped into three categories: the Eucharistic garments, usually worn by the priest or minister; the choir or non-Eucharistic vestments, those articles traditionally worn in the choir or chancel area of the church or outdoors, (they're not vestments per se); and the bishop's regalia. These categories designate who wears what and when, but their categorical lines are fuzzy. A priest may choose to wear a cassock and surplice from the second category along with a stole from the first category to celebrate the Eucharist. The bishop's regalia includes all of the items in the first two categories as well as those listed as specifically episcopal. Some new garments, such as the cassock-alb, combine Eucharistic and choir attire. Other than the distinctive stole, clerical attire is, overall, nonrestrictive and circumstantial.

During the Middle Ages, the clergy created prayers to recite when they ceremonially robed or disrobed. The first seven Eucharistic vestments are described below in the order they are donned, and conclude with their assigned donning prayers. The Vatican II renewal discouraged these prayers. Today, only the most traditional ministers continue to recite them.

Since the garments are described by category and order of use, the following alphabetical index is provided to help locate particular items and terms.

INDEX OF VESTMENTS

THE EUCHARISTIC VESTMENTS
(in the order they are put on)

AMICE

The word "amice" stems from the Latin *amico*, "I wrap around." The white linen rectangular scarf developed from a Roman neck cloth, a *jocale*, worn to protect clothing from sweat as well as to keep the neck warm. Christians adapted it, making it into a head covering for ministers to wear along with the alb. It evolved into a shoulder covering similar to a superhumeral (a jeweled collar of the Byzantine court) before taking its final form as a protective covering around the neck. By the eighth century, when vestment ornamentation became more elaborate, the amice was needed to protect the fragile handwork from contact with skin oils. In the ninth century, ornamented vestments became the norm and the amice became a recognized vestment. With the advent of easy-care fabrics in the twentieth century, and the development of the amiced alb, the amice fell out of common use. Contemporary clergy usually opt for the cassock-alb, which contains an amice, or collar. The cassock-alb offers a clean, neat collar, but it does not provide the overall protection of the amice, so when the neckline becomes soiled, the complete garment—rather than a small piece of cloth—must be laundered.

When the white rectangular scarf is worn, it is the first vestment put on over the cassock or street clothes. The minister places it on the head and secures the amice by crossing its long tapes over the chest and around the waist before tying in front. Once vested, the amice is folded down into its protective position around the neck, often creating a broad collar to the chasuble. The amice ranges in size from its medieval twenty-five by fifty inches to its contemporary range of sixteen to twenty inches by thirty to thirty-six inches with fifty to seventy-two inch tapes. It is adorned with a small red cross embroidered at the center. When an oblong piece of embroidery called an APPAREL is added, the ornament is a stiff three by eight inches and seasonally colored. A longer apparel, up to twenty-six inches, heightens the collar effect (Figure 2–1).

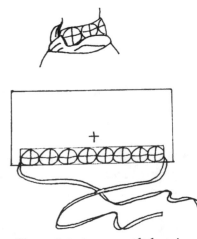

Figure 2-1. An appareled amice.

The following prayer was recited when the amice was positioned on top of the head: "Place, O Lord, the helmet of Salvation upon my head to repel the assaults of the Devil." This prayer reminded clergy of the theological significance of Paul's helmet of salvation from Ephesians 6:11, 17: "Put on the whole armor of God, so that you may be able to stand against the wiles of the devil . . . Take the helmet of salvation."

The ROMAN COLLAR worn with a minister's secular dress derived from the amice. During the Tudor period, the amice was cut down into a neck cloth with long, broad ends. By 1556 this evolved into clerical bands. Over time the broad ends were dropped, leaving a stiff, smooth, wide neck cloth called a *collaro*, which extended from the tunic. Since it was attached to the tunic, a smaller white linen cloth called a *collarino* was used to protect the *collaro* from perspiration. During the seventeenth century, the neck scarf was stylish for gentlemen, and the clergy echoed that trend by fashioning a narrow white collar with a white neck scarf. When the popular neck scarf condensed and evolved into today's neck tie, the clergy dropped the neck scarf and maintained a starched, narrow strip of linen called a "choker," now familiar as a stiff white Roman collar (Figure 2-2).

Figure 2-2.
The Roman collar.

Figure 2-3.
The tunica manicata alba.

ALB

The basic Eucharistic vestment is the alb. "Alb" comes from the Latin *albus*, which means white. In Greek it is *alphos*, white exanthema (white bloom or brilliance bursting forth). The garment derives from the Roman *tunica alba* (white tunic). The *tunica*, a simple undergarment with or without sleeves, of varying length (knee length or longer) and usually girdled, was the common garment of both sexes and all classes of first-century Rome. Its white linen sleeved version, the *tunica manicata alba* (Figure 2-3) was the "proper shirt" of third- and fourth-century statesmen and quickly became the clothing of choice for clergy of the primitive church. Today's traditional, floor-length, long-sleeved, white linen alb resembles its original prototype closely in shape, color, and material.

Initially the alb was worn by any worshiping Christian who could afford the fine white tunic. Gradually it became affiliated with the minor ministers and the newly baptized, who were cloaked in the white robe upon their baptism and wore it daily for the eight days following Easter. On the eighth day, the octave of Easter, the baptized put off their robes, calling the day *Dominica in albis depositis* (the Sunday on which the albs are removed). The practice of dressing the newly baptized in long white garments for the baptismal ceremony continues to the present day.

By the ninth century, the alb became distinctive to ministers—except in Germany, where the laity continued to wear it for at least another century.

The alb has long symbolized holy simplicity and purity as reflected in a variety of biblical texts: the "Ancient One" whose clothing was white as snow (Daniel 7:9); the dazzling white clothes of the transfigured Jesus (Luke 9:29); and, most profoundly, the white robes of the saints in Revelation: "Then one of the elders addressed me saying, 'Who are these, robed in white, and where have they come from?' I said to him, 'Sir, you are the one that knows.' Then he said to me, 'These are they who have come out of the great ordeal; they have washed their robes and made them white in the blood of the Lamb'" (7:13–14).

Because of its predominant use by the clergy, by the early ninth century the alb symbolized the priestly virtues of self-denial and chastity; its floor length served to remind the priest to practice good works to life's end.

By the twelfth century, the SURPLICE supplanted the alb; it was being worn over the cassock. The alb became a Eucharistic garment and began to take on the richness of the other Eucharistic vestments. Fine cloth, color, and lavish ornamentation were used. Apparels, bands of silk, often scarlet and set off with gold fringe, adorned the lower part of the robe and the sleeves. Sometimes lace borders were added around the bottom and the sleeve hems. The lavish ornamentation of this once simple robe was curtailed during the Reformation, when the alb was restored to its original pure white raiment, *alba*, recalling the blessed in heaven.

Today the alb is worn by the ministers, lay and ordained, at the Eucharist. This garment of holy simplicity serves to conceal the street clothes of the ministers and remind them of the sanctity of their work. Currently, a revival of ornamented and colored albs is taking place, but traditionally the alb is white and quite plain. Ornamentation is usually in the form of lace inserted just above the lower and sleeve hemlines. The alb was once donned with the prayer: "Cleanse me, O Lord, and purify my heart, that, being made white in the Blood of the Lamb, I may attain everlasting joy."

CINCTURE/GIRDLE

A belt of some sort is basic to clothing. It holds garments in place and allows for freedom of movement. In the Jewish tradition, the girdle (the *ephod* or Aaron's girdle) designated one as being a priest. It was made of fine twisted linen threads of gold, blue, purple, and scarlet, and was adorned with embroidery and stones.

The girdle or belt image is used in Isaiah's prophecy of the Messiah: "Righteousness shall be the belt around his waist, and faithfulness the belt around his loins" (Isaiah 11:5).

When the tunic or alb took on its floor length, a girdle was essential to facilitate walking with ease. Sometime after the sixth century, when the Romans had abandoned the long *tunica*, and by the ninth century, the girdle became a recognized vestment associated with the Christian Scriptures: "Let your waist be girded and your lamps burning" (Luke 12:35 NKJ) and "Stand therefore, and fasten the belt of truth around your waist" (Ephesians 6:14).

The earliest girdles were actually cinctures, or flat, broad belts fastened with clasps. The usually black broad belt or cincture worn with the cassock today is a direct descendant of the early girdles. The traditional girdle is the simple white, occasionally liturgically colored, twisted linen or cotton cord, one to two inches in circumference, that extends three to five yards in length with a three-to-six-inch tassel or knot on each end. This rope was a common Roman accessory and continues to be used to cinch the alb (Figure 2-4) and to hold the priest's stole in its crossed-over arrangement (see Figure 2-6), although currently the cincture is being abandoned in favor of an ungirded alb. The terms "cincture" and "girdle" are used interchangeably.

Figure 2-4. A girded alb.

Many religious orders wear the cincture as a sign of vows. For example, the Franciscan cincture has three knots tied into its ends that signify the vows of poverty, chastity, and obedience. The cincture worn at Eucharist connotes the minister's spiritual focus on the Lord's service alone. Cinctures have also traditionally symbolized chastity and purity, so the following prayer was commonly said while putting it on: "Gird me, O Lord, with the girdle of purity and quench in me the fire of concupiscence, that the grace of temperance and chastity may abide in me."

STOLE

The long, narrow band the clergy wear around the neck is a stole. The way in which it is worn and its particular style denotes one's office or position (for example, bishop, priest, deacon).

The stole evolved from the Roman *orarium* or *orarion*, a large napkin carried by Roman servants and slaves over the left shoulder that was used to clean a variety of vessels. Sometimes it was worn around the neck like a scarf in order to wipe dust from the mouth and to dry off sweat. In the early church, the deacon carried the *orarium* to clean the Eucharistic vessels and to wipe the minister's face and hands. Later, when the emperor began to use the *orarium* to signal the beginning of the games and for applause during the games, the bishop adopted the stole to signify his authority. The deacon imitated the emperor's action by using the *orarium* to alert the priest and the laity to perform certain actions. By the seventh century in the south and by the eleventh century in the north, the *orarium*, worn around the neck by priests and bishops or over the left shoulder by deacons, was given to all orders of the clergy at the time of ordination.

How the name changed from *orarium* to "stole" is a bit of a mystery, since a *stola* anciently referred to a woman's garment similar to the man's *tunica*. It may come from the Latin Vulgate's use of the word "stole" rather than "robe" in the text of Revelation 7:14, "the saints are clothed in white stoles," making the word "stole" a reference to the vestments as a whole during the Middle Ages.[6] Amalarius (circa 780–850) the Bishop of Metz and a liturgical scholar, discovered that the Gallican church referred to the *orarium* as a stole, and he did the same. By the tenth century the Roman church adopted the term "stole," and the word came into general use by the twelfth century. In the Eastern church, the priest's stole is called an *epitrachelion*; the deacon's stole continues to be called by its original appellation, *orarion*.

Simultaneous with the name change was the revision of the stole's form from a large folded napkin to a narrow (two to six inches) adorned long strip with occasional widening at the ends. The stole remained relatively plain until the eighth century, when adornments of gold and bells became popular. Modifications to the stole's width, ranging from one uniform width to a narrowing at the neck and a widening at the ends—which broadened into a spade shape—occurred during the eighteenth century (Figure 2-5). Colors also varied from a striking contrast to an exact match with the chasuble. The sixteenth century affixed three embroidered crosses to the stole, a "kissing cross" at the center back and one at each end, that became requisite during the nineteenth century and lasted until the mid-twentieth century. When the Protestants of the Reformation discarded vestments in general, a black scarf known as the canon's scarf remained in use.

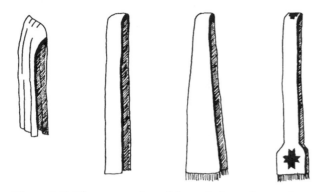

Figure 2-5. The progression of the stole from the orarium *to the spaded ends.*

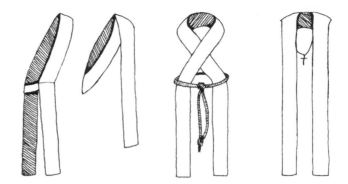

Figure 2-6. How the stole is worn (from left to right): Western style deacon's stole, Eastern style deacon's stole, the priest's stole, the bishop's stole.

The continued use of this scarf made it simple to reintroduce the stole during the liturgical revival of the 1800s, although it too remained black for a while.

How the Stole Is Worn

In order to keep the right arm free for service, a deacon wears his or her stole over the left shoulder and across the breast to a right-side closure at the hip. This style was codified by the Council of Toledo in 633 and is maintained in the West. In the East, the deacon's *orarion* is worn crossed over the left shoulder, with the ends falling down the left side before and behind the torso. Currently, deacons in the West wear both styles of stole.

Traditionally, the priest places the stole around the neck and, when worn with an alb, crosses it in front before cinching it in place with the cincture, as determined by the Council at Braga in 675. When worn with an ungirded alb, a surplice, or over the chasuble, the stole falls straight down the front. In the East, the priest's *epitrachelion* consists of a broad strip of material with a hole at one end for the head to slip through, much like a seamed Western stole would appear. In the

West, this type of stole is called a *pallium* stole and may have a corresponding long strip hanging down the back (Figure 2-7).

The bishop's stole hangs straight from the neck to frame the pectoral cross worn over the breast.

Types of Stoles

The Eucharistic stole is long enough to be crossed and to show below the chasuble, around 90–112" long by 3–5" wide.

Since the preaching stole is usually worn uncrossed with a surplice, it is about ten inches shorter than the Eucharistic stole, so as to not go below the surplice, and it is somewhat wider at its ends. It ranges from 80" to 94" long (knee length) by 5–9" across at both ends and tapers to 3–4½" at the neck. A tasseled cord may be attached along its inner edge to secure the stole across the breast.

The pocket stole is used for visitations, making it much smaller and convenient to carry. It measures 56–72" long by 2" wide and is reversible, using the same colors as the baptismal stole (see below).

The confessional stole is about 100" long by 2½–3" wide, worked in violet with simple gold crosses.

The visitation stole is a white variation of the confessional stole.

The baptismal stole is eighteen inches shorter than the confessional stole and is reversible, with the confessional stole on one side and the visitation stole on the other. It is worn pendant style for ease in switching the color. The minister wears the purple side out—to symbolize the soul's condition of original sin—until the renewal of the baptismal covenant, when the stole is switched to the white side to symbolize purification.

An overlay stole with a fitted cape back is worn over the other vestments, including the chasuble. The front tails measure around 5" wide by 48" long.

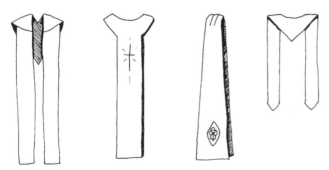

Figure 2-7. Other types of stoles (from left to right): the overlay stole, the pallium *stole, the tippet or scarf, a choir stole.*

The *pallium* hangs in a single 8" wide piece and is about 44" long down the front and back.

The deacon wears the *stolone* or broad stole at a solemn High Mass. When used, the deacon processes in a *stolone*, around 110" long by 8–10" wide, worn in same fashion as other diaconal stoles. The deacon exchanges a chasuble for the *stolone* before proclaiming the Gospel and before the post-communion prayer.

The choir is a modified, simple stole worn by members of the choir to mark the liturgical seasons. It is usually short, reversible, and worn backwards, with the ends hanging down the back.

Today, the stole is made in a variety of styles and colors that may or may not match the other Eucharistic appointments, but it is always recognizable as the emblem of ordination. It symbolizes the cross of Christ and the yoke of service, particularly the sacraments. Traditionally, each order bears the cross. The deacon's stole, crossed at the shoulder so that it slashes across the body, is a reminder of the cost of discipleship and is a sign of his or her call to serve in the world. When worn crossed over the breast, the priest's stole is a sign of Christ always leading and being central in his or her heart. Worn pendant style, the bishop's stole flanks the pectoral cross, the cross of authority and unity.

During vesting, the stole prayer was: "Give me again, O Lord, the stole of immortality, which I lost by the transgression of my first parents, and although I am unworthy to come unto Thy Holy Sacrament, grant that I may attain everlasting felicity."

The STOLE COLLAR is a narrow strip of linen, ten to twelve inches by two inches folded over, which is basted inside the neck of the stole to protect it from skin oils.

MANIPLE

The nearly obsolete maniple is a small edition of the stole worn over the left forearm. It replaced the basic function of the stole when the stole became too ornate for its utilitarian purpose. The maniple began as a plain white linen napkin used for wiping the clergy's hands and face, and was carried in the left hand since pockets did not yet exist. Inconvenient to hold, in the eleventh century the maniple gave way to being displayed over the left forearm in imitation of a table attendant's napkin (Figure 2-8). It was called by many names: a *mappulla* (napkin), a *mantile* (handkerchief), a *sudarium* (sweat cloth), or a *fanon* or *phanon* (a flag or ensign). An alternative to the *orarium*, the latter name derived from the handkerchief the consul held in his right hand and threw down to signal the beginning of the games, and provided a mark of dignity to the garment. A prevalent medieval name was

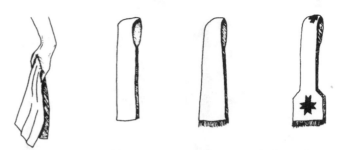

Figure 2-8. The development of the maniple from the hand-held mappulla *to the spaded ends.*

sudarium, since this kerchief was originally used to wipe the sweat off the minister's face. The word had symbolic meaning because the *sudarium* was the legendary napkin Veronica used to wipe the sweat from Jesus as he carried the cross, miraculously leaving an imprint of his face on the napkin. By the tenth century the maniple symbolized the sacred calling of ministry.

Like the stole, the maniple began as a large cloth folded or rolled into a long, narrow shape. Eventually, around 1000 C.E., its size and shape were reduced to a narrow band ranging from thirty-six to forty-four inches long by two to four inches wide and caught at its sides six inches down from center—or it had a loop attached to hold it in place. It was carried by priests of the early church and by bishops and deacons by the ninth century. In the eleventh century, subdeacons added it to their apparel. During the ninth and eighteenth centuries, acolytes and choir boys wore the maniple. Over time the maniple, like the stole, lost its utilitarian function, becoming richly adorned with expensive fabrics, especially silks, and embroidery.

The clergy of the Eastern church do not wear maniples. The item closest to the maniple that they do use is a square ornament hung from the cincture on the right side called an *epigonation*. In the West, clergy have all but abandoned this purely ceremonial garment because the maniple is bothersome to wear and can easily fall forward into the chalice during a service, causing the wine to spill. Those who still use it do so out of symbolic piety for the servant's napkin. It reminds the wearer that he or she is primarily a servant of Christ and of the people. The vesting prayer for this garment was: "Grant me, O Lord, to bear the light burden of grief and sorrow, that I may with gladness take the reward of my labor."

CHASUBLE

The sleeveless, conspicuous outer garment worn by the priest at celebrations of the Eucharist derived from the Roman *paenula* or *planeta*, a long leather or woolen sleeveless cloak, usually with a hood, worn by everyone for protection from the weather. The Romans were punctilious about dress and distinguished between the *paenula* of the poor, the toga worn by Roman citizens, and the *chlamys*, the short cloak worn by soldiers. While accessible to all first-century Romans, the *paenula* was typically the garment of the lower classes; it was used by the upper classes only in bad weather.

Roman citizens took a fancy to the *paenula* during the fourth century and it became the fashion, replacing the toga. They wore it over the *tunica* along with a scarf color-coded according to rank. By the sixth century, this ensemble was prestigious. So, during the first six hundred years of Christianity, the *paenula* gained respectability, evolving from a garment worn by the poor to one worn by the elite. The church followed suit as it gained status too, developing from a persecuted church in solidarity with the poor to an institution affiliated with the state, whose leaders were accepted among the gentry. That the clergy continued to wear the same garments throughout the six hundred-year period is a natural consequence of these simultaneous transitions. During the first centuries, all ministers wore the *paenula*, but by the sixth century it was becoming recognized as a garment solely for the ordained. By the tenth century it was specific to bishops and priests.

In its earliest form, the *paenula* was a circular or rectangular shape with a hole in the middle for the head. The garment fell in wide folds around the whole body, giving it its familiar name, chasuble, from the Latin *casula*, "hut" or "little house." (The Eastern church uses the name *phelonion* from the Greek *phelones*, the word used to refer to Paul's cloak in 2 Timothy 4:13.) A style adopted in the early Middle Ages was bell-shaped, made from a semicircular piece of cloth with the cut edges closed up the front; the top section cut away to allow for an opening for the head. Both styles of the garment proved highly impractical for the celebration of the liturgy, because the large folds had to be gathered to free the hands to perform the Eucharistic action. Out of necessity, the deacon held up the sides of the chasuble to free the priest's hands. The solemn High Mass rite of the deacon lifting the back of the priest's chasuble during the prayer of consecration comes from the bygone need to hold the cumbersome chasuble out of the way.

Over time, the chasuble was opened and shortened on the sides while maintaining its length to give a less cumbersome oval form. By the sixteenth century, the sides were cut away entirely to introduce a shield shape, rich with embroidery. Another style in use by the tenth century featured a long back with a short, pointed front. Following the tenth century, the chasuble was subject to many changes in color and style. The extreme reduction in size produced the continental, scant fiddle-backed chasuble (see Figure 2-9).

The earliest chasubles were plain, usually made from white wool, often open in the front. Typically the chasuble was closed with a broach at the neckline that served as the only frontal embellishment; it later developed into the cope's MORSE. When closed, the ample circular garment created folds when the priest's arms were lifted, leaving only the area around the neck smooth. The convergence of these folds just below the neck may have inspired the favored and richly embroidered "flower" ornaments placed at the breast and at the upper part of back. In addition, the seam that closed the front of the chasuble was concealed with a braid extending the length of the front; it came to be called an orphrey. As time went by, the needlework on orphreys became increasingly more exquisite, until, during the twelfth century, the Y-cross orphrey enhanced or replaced the flower ornament. The fourteenth century favored chasubles with a straight Latin cross orphrey on the back and a straight broad stripe down the front called a pillar. Occasionally, the Y or the Latin cross was placed on the front and the back. The contemporary chasuble is designed and adorned in countless ways. Many of those who design chasubles aim to imitate the ancient, full style and its dignity of roundness, yet with streamlined or open sides that prevent the garment from becoming cumbersome and binding.

The Middle Ages imbued the chasuble with its symbolism as a sacrificial robe. The reformers rejected such symbolism and referred to the chasuble simply as "the vestment," since it was the one article visible in its entirety to the people. These different interpretations caused some confusion with vestments in general, which included the amice, alb, cincture, stole, maniple, and chasuble. For example, controversy still exists as to whether the rubric in the 1549 English Book of Common Prayer calls for a chasuble alone or a combination of pieces (see page 7). The enduring sacrificial symbolism has caused some Protestants to shy away from using a chasuble, while other ministers wait until after the liturgy of the Word to put on the chasuble for the Great Thanksgiving. Other ministers still maintain the tradition of wearing the chasuble for the entire Eucharistic celebration. A contemporary variation is the CHASUBLE-ALB, which functions as an all-in-one garment by consolidating the alb's color (white or neutral), the amice's neckline (hood), and

Figure 2-9. The Evolution of the Chasuble.

First-century paenula

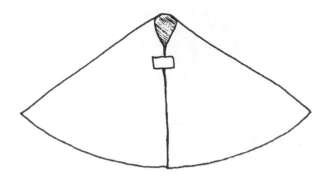

Eleventh-century conical

*Tenth-century short
front variation*

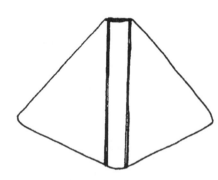

*Twelfth-century bell shape
with front pillar*

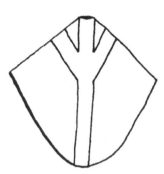

*Fourteenth-century Roman
with "Y" cross*

*Sixteenth-century board
with Latin cross*

*Seventeenth-century
fiddle-back*

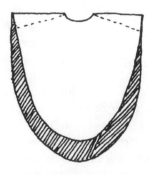

*Twentieth century with
alternate shoulder taper*

the chasuble (a full, sleeved form), leaving only the stole (worn on top) to complete the ensemble.

The prayer at vesting includes the "amen," because the chasuble is the last vestment put on: "O Lord, who hast said, 'My yoke is easy, and My burden is light,' grant that I may so bear it, as to attain Thy grace. Amen."

DALMATIC

This garment is worn loosely over an alb by the deacon at a choral High Mass. It is a knee-length tunic with elbow-length sleeves ornamented with two vertical orphreys and two horizontal apparels.

*Figure 2-10.
The* dalmatica.

The *dalmatica*, an ungirded wool tunic with three-quarter-length sleeves, was introduced to Rome from Dalmatia around 190 C.E. It became popular among the Roman gentry by the third century and was adorned with the *clavi* characteristic of the *tunica* (Figure 2-10).

Pope Sylvester I (314–335) designated the dalmatic as the diaconal vestment to replace the *colobium* in the early fourth century (Figure 1-7). The *colobium*, a close-fitting tunic commonly worn by the privileged Romans and senators, was used as the burial garment for martyrs and worn by deacons to connote true servanthood of Christ. The early dalmatic was white linen or wool adorned with Tyrian purple *clavi*. This early and simple form is evident in the frescoes of the catacombs. While the dalmatic took on varying degrees of fullness and ornamentation over the years, with a longer tunic preferred during the Middle Ages, little has changed over the centuries other than its color. By the ninth century, the bishops had assumed the dalmatic, and many priests wore it under their chasuble. During the twelfth century, the deacon's dalmatic could be discerned by its needleworked apparels, which favored scenes from the life of St. Stephen.

Seldom used today, a dalmatic need not be identical in color and ornamentation to the chasuble; however, it is made to harmonize with the chasuble and the liturgical season. Adornment is as varied as current chasubles, only simpler. The prayer said while donning the dalmatic was: "O Lord, clothe me with the garment of Salvation, and cover me with the robe of righteousness."

TUNICLE

The dalmatic and tunicle are counterparts of the celebrant's chasuble. The bishop wore both under his chasuble; the deacon wore the dalmatic; and the subdeacon, acolytes, and other minor clerics wore a tunicle. The tunicle, if used, is worn by the subdeacon at solemn High Mass. It is slightly shorter and plainer than the dalmatic. Initially it was unadorned; later, two vertical orphreys with one horizontal apparel were added. Basically, the dalmatic and tunicle are the same garment, differing only by their apparels. The variation in the stripes follows the Roman practice of varying the *clavi* to distinguish rank. The simple garment for the subdeacon was designed to affiliate the subdeacon with the other Eucharistic ministers, while simultaneously designating lesser status than the deacon. The dalmatic and tunicle are not worn in the East. There the assistant ministers wear an alb (*stoicharion*) and the deacon adds a stole.

Pope Gregory the Great (circa 540–604) recommended the tunicle be abandoned for the white alb, but by the twelfth century the tunicle was reinstated for all servers to wear. In the fourteenth century it was again restricted to the subdeacon. It may be appropriate for a lay Eucharistic minister to wear the tunicle when the deacon wears the dalmatic. The same vesting prayer is said for the tunicle as for the dalmatic.

HUMERAL VEIL

The humeral veil is a broad, rectangular cut of fabric, some 2½–3 yards long by 20–27 inches wide, corresponding to the vestments traditionally worn by the subdeacon during the solemn High Mass. It is worn over the shoulders, extends to cover the hands, and is used to hold—within its folds and to avoid touching them—the paten and chalice while they are transported to the altar. The priest may use it during the Benediction to shield the foot of the monstrance (the vessel that holds the consecrated bread) while it is being held. Its purpose is to prevent the hands of the ministers from touching the sacred vessels, an instruction that may come from the mandate in Numbers 4:15: "[T]he Kohathites shall come to carry these, but they must not touch the holy things, or they will die." The veil, originally of white linen and called a *velum subdiaconale*, subdeacon's veil, was in use as early as the second century. Because it was used to wrap the Eucharistic elements, by the Middle Ages it was symbolic of Christ's winding sheet.

Burse

From the Latin *bursa* (sac or pouch, especially of skin) the burse is a square, firm pocket used to carry the folded corporal and extra purificators to and from the altar.[7] The burse prevents them from becoming soiled. It is made to match the vestments, lined with linen or silk, and stiffened with cardboard. When the burse came into liturgical use is unknown, but it is relatively recent. The corporal cloth, which it houses, initially spanned the length of the altar. When the bread was reduced in quantity and from full-size loaves to small hosts, the corporal was also reduced in size from around twenty inches square and was carried in a missal or box that evolved into the burse. From the fourteenth century onward, the burse gained in popularity; it was generally in use by the seventeenth century.

Chalice Veil

This is a square, lined cloth, made and ornamented similarly to its germane vestments. The veil originated with the medieval practice of concealing the sacred vessels while they were carried to and from the

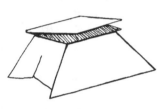

*Figure 2-11.
Chalice veil and burse.*

altar. It is about twenty-four inches square, but varies according to the height of the chalice it covers. The burse and the chalice veil are regarded as "vestments" because they vest the corporal and chalice (Figure 2-11).

Paraments

While they are not vestments, paraments are ordinarily made to coordinate with the vestments. Paraments are the ornamental hangings used for worship and include the pulpit scarf, the Bible markers, and the *antependium* or altar frontal. Each of these ornamented cloths is used to enhance the worship space by adding color and symbolism. They also draw the worshipers' attention to the stations of import: the pulpit, the lectern, and the altar. Initially, altars were completely draped in rich cloth, but when they were placed against the wall during the Middle Ages, the drapes were reduced to richly ornamented bands extending across the front of the altar. In contemporary churches, the altar is endowed with a variety of cloths ranging from stoles to a full covering, although some altars are left plain. The architectural setting, shape, placement, substance, and adornment of the altar all help to center the worshipers' attention. If paraments are used, they should complete and

enhance the worship space rather than dominate the space or distract worshipers.

The Choir Attire

Cassock

The black, floor-length, long-sleeved, close-fitting robe worn primarily by liturgically oriented ministers, lay and ordained, in the West and in the East, is called a cassock. A modest garment, it covers the body from the neck to the feet and typically closes in front with a series of small buttons (see Figure 2-12). The cassock evolved from the *caracalla*, a close-fitting, long-sleeved, short undergarment worn in Gaul and Rome (Figure 2-13) and the *byrrus*, a heavy, woolen, cowled cape of first-century Rome (Figure 1-2). The fashionable long black robe became the daily wear of Roman dignitaries and senior citizens from the third through the seventh centuries. The clergy adopted the style for their daily secular wear when the fashion was abandoned by the Romans. During the Middle Ages, they were often lined with fur for warmth.

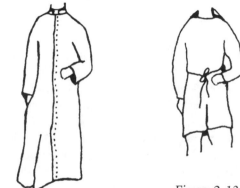

Figure 2-12. The cassock.

*Figure 2-13.
The* caracalla.

By the tenth century in the East and the sixteenth century in the West, the clergy began to use a black garment for secular wear. Even when it was worn under the Eucharistic vestments, the cassock never attained the status of a vestment because it functioned primarily as everyday dress. Eventually the cassock followed contemporary trends in fashion and evolved into the clerical black suit. However, the cassock still prevails among the clergy for worship services and for the laity as an alternative to the alb for all liturgies.

Since the cassock was not restricted to the clergy, colors that distinguished the orders of ministers were adopted quite early. Traditional cassock colors include: white for the Pope; scarlet or black trimmed in scarlet for cardinals; purple or black trimmed in purple for bishops; black for priests and deacons. A canon[8] traditionally wears a black cassock piped with the cathedral's color. Lay readers and choir members traditionally wear black; purple if they serve at a cathedral church. Junior choir cassock colors are black, blue, or red; acolyte colors are black or red, purple at a cathedral. Monks traditionally wear cassocks depending on the color of the habit of their order. Today, the color specifications are not necessarily observed, making the rank of a minister in a cassock less evident. A new garment, the CASSOCK-ALB, combines the cassock form with the alb color (white) and the amice "collar." It may be worn girded and with a stole and/or chasuble, by all ministers, lay and ordained.

SURPLICE

This is an ample white overgarment, as opposed to the alb, which is a white undergarment. The surplice is a knee-length, ungirded garment with a gathered yoke and large, full sleeves that may be round or pointed (Figure 2-14). The large sleeves originally served to protect the service books from moisture.

Figure 2-14.
The surplice.

The surplice began as a choir vestment and was worn over (*super*) the characteristic fur-lined clothing (*pellicae* or cassock) of northern Europe for processions and burials from perhaps as early as the eleventh century. The narrow, girded alb proved impractical for the clergy of the north; they needed an ample, ungirded garment that would easily fit over their heavy fur clothing. Gradually, the surplice began to be used throughout Christendom, with multiple modifications over the years.

Currently, the surplice is worn by clergy and lay ministers over the cassock; since the sixteenth century it has been ornamented with inserted bands of lace. It is used for processions and all non-Eucharistic services. It may be worn at the Eucharist when a stole is added, which was the practice in the Anglican Communion from the mid-sixteenth through the mid-nineteenth centuries, albeit without the stole.

COTTA

This vestment may have begun as a synonym for "surplice" and is worn by lay ministers over the cassock. It has evolved into a short white garment fashioned after the surplice but with less overall length and fullness.

GENEVA GOWN

This black academic gown is worn as a Protestant pulpit robe. The academic gown was adapted from the monastic habit because monasticism was the center of learning during the Middle Ages. In the sixteenth century John Calvin adopted the scholar's gown. It soon became the accepted dress for clergy during the Reformation, except for Roman Catholics, who maintained their traditional dress, and Puritans, who protested all distinctive clergy attire. The continental Geneva gown evolved into a gown with narrower sleeves than the English academic gown. A variation of the gown is worn by vergers (lay attendants, interior caretakers, or sextons).

BANDS

The bands are the two strips of white linen, six to eight inches long, which hang from the collar of the Geneva gown below the chin. The Protestant clerical and legal profession in the seventeenth and eighteenth centuries adopted them to symbolize the tablets or Law of Moses.

TIPPET

Sometimes called a preaching scarf, the tippet is a wide black stole-like scarf worn over a surplice for non-Eucharistic occasions. It ranges from six to eight inches wide by about three yards long. Its width is tapered with three pleats at the neck for fit. It stems from the cape section of the medieval university hood, the *almuce*, and its ends feature church or school emblems (see Figure 2-7).

HOOD

Another derivative from the medieval university hood or *almuce*, the hood hangs from the neck and extends down the back. The silk lining inside the hood is colored to denote the degree-granting university; the velvet band denotes the field of study; and the length, the academic degree. It may be worn with the tippet.

ALMUCE

A fur hood with a small cape attached evolved during the thirteenth century into a choir habit worn over the surplice for protection from the cold (Figure 2-15). Sometimes called a "furred amys," the quality of the *almuce's* fur designated hierarchical status. The tails of the animal's fur were sometimes hung from the shoulders like pendants. The *almuce* became obsolete when it evolved into the university hood and the tippet.

Figure 2-15.
The almuce.

HEADGEAR

Before the thirteenth century, the clergy were forbidden to wear headgear in church. Due to the cold in the unheated churches and the unprotected tonsured head, Pope Innocent IV allowed the monks to wear their habit hoods, *almuces*, during the Offices (prayers) or services. Shortly thereafter, the clergy adopted headgear for warmth and protection. A number of styles of headgear developed over the years, some of which continue to be in use today. The most common are listed below.

The SQUARE CAP became a popular and recognized clergy cap during the sixteenth century. Its top grew wider over the years, and by the nineteenth century it developed into the college mortarboard.

The BIRETTA, from the Latin *birrus* (hood) is a rigid, square cap with three (clerk) to four (doctor) points and a pompon projecting from its crown. Its points developed from the fourteenth-century, supple, pointed woolen skullcap (*pileus*) which retained the indentations created by the fingers when it was put on or taken off. Originally for outdoor services, this fifteenth-century cap is worn nowadays for processions and informal services. The biretta follows the same color scheme as the cassock (Figure 2-16).

The SKULLCAP is a tight-fitting round cap composed of eight triangular pieces; it was adopted by the clergy during the thirteenth century as a warm covering over the tonsure. Heated churches, instead of cold ones, made it into a sign of dignity. The black skullcap for priests is called a COIF, the episcopal cap is a ZUCHETTO.

Figure 2-16. The biretta and the skullcap.

THE BISHOP'S *PONTIFICALIA*

ROCHET

This is a white variation of the alb, except it is worn ungirded under the chimere and is far more ample. The rochet is gathered at the neck; at the wrists, it has a ruffle adorned with an apparel to coordinate with the chimere. The rochet began as a narrow-sleeved or sleeveless garment for minor ministers, cantors, and children. Eventually the clergy adopted it until the fifteenth-century, when its use was restricted to bishops. The abundant sleeves were added after the Reformation (Figure 2-17).

Figure 2-17.
The rochet and chimere.

Figure 2-18.
The mozetta.

CHIMERE

A sleeveless, open-faced black or red academic gown worn over the rochet and of the same length as the rochet. Of Spanish origin, the chimere developed during the Middle Ages from the *zamarra*, a short sleeveless sheepskin cloak. When presiding at the liturgy, the bishop may wear the rochet and the chimere in place of an alb and chasuble or cope. In either case, a stole and pectoral cross are worn to complete the vestment.

SCARF

The bishop's scarf is a longer version of the tippet and is usually adorned with the bishop's diocesan emblem at the ends. The extra length stems from the early church practice of using more length to denote status. It may be worn in place of the stole (see Figure 2-7).

MOZETTA

A shortened chimere, the mozetta developed from the Spanish *zamarra* and the *almuce* into a short hoodless cape (Figure 2-18). The mozetta designated privilege. It is colored according to rank and is worn by some religious orders.

MITRE

The bishop's flame-shaped hat reaches approximately thirteen inches high with two cloven points. The mitre stems from the Roman *camelaucum*, a cone-shaped cap that adorned the episcopacy by the eighth century (Figure 2-19). The Anglo-Saxons used a linen headdress with

Figure 2-19.
The camelaucum *and mitre.*

long ends that fell to shoulders under the band of gold. By the late tenth century, the mitre took its definite form as an amalgamation of these early hats, complete with bands suspended from the back to hold the mitre on the head. These evolved into the decorative bands called *infulae* or FANONS that hang from the mitre down the back. The mitre gained its liturgical status in the twelfth century, but its form was modified in height and shape until the sixteenth-century, when it grew into a cumbersome costume. The 1800s revived the version we know today, which was its fourteenth-century style. A plain white mitre is called a SIMPLEX MITRE.

COPE

An ornamental processional cape, the cope may be worn by anyone but is typically reserved for a bishop. It was a distinctive ecclesiastical dress by the sixth century; by the twelfth century it gained its large clasp, called a morse, for closure at the neck. The cope shares its origins with the chasuble, stemming from the open-front *paenula* (see Figure 1-3). Unlike the chasuble it has retained the hood, which has evolved into a decorative shield that hangs down between the shoulders and varies in shape (Figure 2-20). A Gothic hood is smaller and pointed and a Roman hood is wider and rounded. The late Middle Ages conferred symbolism on all the cope's details. Because it resembles an inverted Gothic arch, the hood represents the joy of heaven. The orphrey reaches to the feet because we must persevere in good living to the end. The fringe reminds the wearer that his or her labor consummates the service of God. The open front is a reminder that eternal life lies open to the ministers of Christ who lead a holy life.[9]

Figure 2-20. The cope, front and back view.

The BLACK CAPE is nearly identical to its dark woolen ancestor, the first century *paenula*, later called *cappa* by ecclesiastics. It has retained its hood and is used for outdoor processions and services by all orders of ministers, as well as for general warmth.

The *cappa magna* is an ample cope with train worn in the Roman church by the Pope, cardinals, and other high dignitaries. Its color matches the cassock over which it is worn.

BUSKINS

From the Greek use of cloth to wrap the legs and feet, buskins are liturgical, knee-high, colored stockings worn by the episcopacy since the seventeenth century.

SANDALS

Sandals are slippers designed to wear over buskins for Mass. The development of a liturgical shoe began as early as the fifth century.

GLOVES

Worn to keep the hands warm and to avoid touching the sacred elements, gloves gained liturgical status during the twelfth century.

PECTORAL CROSS

Wearing a cross from a chain that hangs over one's breast is a personal devotional matter. Sometimes, a particular cross serves as an ensign to a religious order and, in the case of vestments, a large, usually ornate gold or silver cross is used to designate a bishop, particularly when it is worn flanked by the bishop's stole (see Figure 2-6).

Young Roman boys wore a *bulla*, an ornament worn around the neck for protection from evil or as a distinguishing ornament of citizenry. Bishops began to wear small devotional objects during the third century. This in turn became popular with the laity during the fourth century after the discovery of the "True Cross" in 326 by St. Helena. Slivers of the cross were enclosed in gold for wearing. An evolving and abiding love for the cross generated the varietal cross, worn by countless Christians since the Middle Ages.

The large pectoral cross, from the Latin *pectus*, "breast," became a common accessory among the Eastern bishops by the tenth century. It became an acknowledged vestment specific to the office of bishop during the fourteenth century. The pectoral cross serves to remind the bishop to keep the cross of Christ before him or her. Because the stole worn by priests and deacons represents the cross by the way it is worn, they do not need the accessory.

CROZIER

At the church's beginnings, bishops were few and poor. They were forced to travel great distances by foot. Naturally, they habitually carried a walking stick and were granted the unique privilege of leaning on their staff during the reading of the Gospel. With prosperity, the bishops were able to take on the Roman *scipio*, a dignified, finely crafted staff carried by the elite.

The crozier took on liturgical significance by the seventh century, and its curved top appeared at the turn of the second millennium. The crozier symbolically incorporated the pastoral crook of the good shepherd, the staff of authority, the rod of defense against evil, the spike to spur on the weak, and the support of the Gospel for the Christian life.

RING

Rings have long been worn as ornaments, seals, and symbols of rank. The ring was adopted to denote a bishop's civil status in fourth-century Rome. Styles ranged from extremely simple to outrageously ornate; some contained a relic. Worn on the third finger of the right hand, the bishop's ring symbolizes the bishop's spiritual marriage to the church and willingness to lay down his or her life for the church. By tradition, clergy and lay people bow and kiss the ring as a sign of respect.

GREMIALE

A thirty-four inch square lap cloth is used to cover the lap and knees while the bishop is seated during the Mass. It originated for all ministers to use in order to protect the vestments from their dirty hands, a common medieval problem.

PALLIUM

The arch-episcopal badge is a narrow (three fingers wide) circle of lamb's wool, laid over the shoulders with an equally wide strip of lamb's wool hanging down front and rear as far as the knees. The wool of the Western *pallium* comes from lambs whose wool is designated and blessed for the purpose.

The Roman *pallium* was an adaptation of the Greek *himation*, a large, rectangular outer garment worn by men, women (*palla*) and children. Worn alone, it was the characteristic garment of the philosopher and scholar and the mantle of Christ (see Figure 1-1).

SUBCINGULUM

A second girdle developed into a maniple-type cloth that is suspended from the left side of the pope's girdle when he celebrates the Eucharist. All celebrants wore the *subcingulum* until the ninth century, when Pope Innocent III retained it for the Pope's exclusive use and made it symbolic of almsgiving and apostolic power (Figure 2-21).

*Figure 2-21.
The* subcingulum.

NOTES

3.
ELEMENTS OF UNITY:
ON MATTERS OF DESIGN

*Three things are needed for beauty: wholeness,
harmony and radiance.*

—Thomas Aquinas

Beauty radiates harmony. As designers and makers of vestments, we are commissioned to create garments that are harmonious and beautiful, simple and graceful, balanced and enduring. The principles of design help us to recognize integrity of shape, a harmonious rhythm of motifs and proportion, and a variety of texture and color.

Vestment designers are able to envision how their creations will integrate into the worship service and the church. The overall concept for a vestment is obviously important to the design, but the arrangement of its pieces, including any ornamentation, contributes as well. The goal of vestment design is to create a harmonious effect, giving full expression to the materials used, engaging the interest of the worshiping community, and relating the vestments to the order and vitality of liturgy. A clear and simple design will result in a vestment that functions well, from a solitary stole to a complete traditional set. As you work up your design, consider the principles of unity, balance, rhythm, variety, and form. Understanding these guidelines will strengthen your project from inception to completion.

THE PRINCIPLES OF DESIGN

Unity

Seek to unify your project within the worship environment and within itself. All of the pieces are interrelated and should reflect, through an overall organization, a balanced, satisfying quality of oneness. Unity does not dictate that all the pieces must be the same, but when the pieces contrast, they should still convey an underlying unity and mutual interdependence. The overarching unity comes from the liturgy. Vestments are part of a larger whole, reflecting the liturgy's commanding unity. The liturgy consists of prayer, proclamation, and the Great Thanksgiving, which take place in a particular place on a particular date. Vestments harmonize with the liturgy in ways that are identifiable, symbolic, and mysterious. When you design a vestment, keep in mind its role in the liturgy. Vestments should accentuate the worship environment, not overwhelm it. If they become the focus of the event, they do not serve their purpose.

Balance

One way to achieve unity is through balance, the arrangement of all the elements involved into a cohesive whole. To create balance, repeat color, ornamentation, texture, and shape; then contrast those elements with accents of brighter colors, striking ornaments, textural changes, and the variety of pieces in a vestment set. The formality of the vestments is influenced by different types of balance. When all the elements work together symmetrically (everything is mirrored down an imaginary center line) the vestments will tend toward formality, while an asymmetrical placement of color and adornment will look more informal. A design that radiates from the center and gathers the pieces into its orb is in radial or circular balance (Figure 3-1). Since it is circular, the chasuble lends itself well to a radial design.

Figure 3-1. The types of balance: symmetry, asymmetry, radial.

Rhythm

Built into the liturgy is a rhythm of proclamation and response. The holy rhythm of worship can be echoed by the vestments; they too, create a rhythm. Theirs is a visual rhythm that complements through line, shape, color, and pattern. A good vestment design is based on some sort of rhythm that blends all the vestment pieces into a related whole.

Variety

Variety is rhythm's companion. The liturgical seasons and their vestments lend variety to the liturgical year. The assorted garments' color, size, shape, texture, and line all add variety, which also can be enhanced or minimized by ornamentation. Trims and colors may be arranged into a repetitious pattern or may vary from piece to piece. Repeating symbols or retaining them as a solitary focus also adds rhythm and variety. Some motifs may repeat on each piece but vary by size and placement.

Form

The vestment ensemble is composed of a number of forms with individual characteristics. By form we mean the shape and size of each article as well as the volume created once the article is put on. Off the body, the vestments are flattened forms of varying shapes and sizes; once donned, they acquire depth and movement. A stole may be worn crossed, folded over the shoulder, or hanging straight down. It may be used alone, over, or under a chasuble. The wearer may be short or tall, thin or overweight, erect or hunched. Vestments conform to the body and are viewed from all angles. The shape of the wearer and the many points of view generated by his or her movement create an interplay with the surrounding space and its accoutrements. Not only the person who wears the vestments, but also where the vestments are worn can affect their form. When possible, consider these variables when you design vestments.

THE ELEMENTS OF DESIGN

The elements of vestment design include size and shape, line and ornamentation, texture and fabric, and color. These ingredients are used to sustain design. Some elements, such as shape, color, and ornamentation, are associated with distinct symbols, while other elements are basic instruments of the craft.

Size and Shape

Proportion and emphasis are achieved through size and shape. The relationship of the vestments to the worship environment as well as their correspondence to each other punctuate and influence the use of color, fabric, and ornamentation. The ample size of the chasuble emphasizes the key participant and lends unity to the smaller pieces. Because it is large, the chasuble may require less brilliance than the stole, for example. Since the stole is relatively small, it may need stunning color and ornamentation to emphasize the person wearing it, especially if a chasuble is not worn. A spacious, plain church welcomes a more radiant design than a small, lavish environment. Size and shape support and unify the vestment pieces, the human form, and the surrounding space.

The traditional vestment model uses an ideal set of proportional ratios based on the average male human body. This traditional scale, combined with the measurements of the wearer when available, determines the actual size of the individual garments. A standard stole is approximately three yards long. For a petite person it may need to be shortened, while it will need to be lengthened for a tall or heavyset person. The size of the ornaments is affected by the size and role of a particular vestment and by how much of the piece and

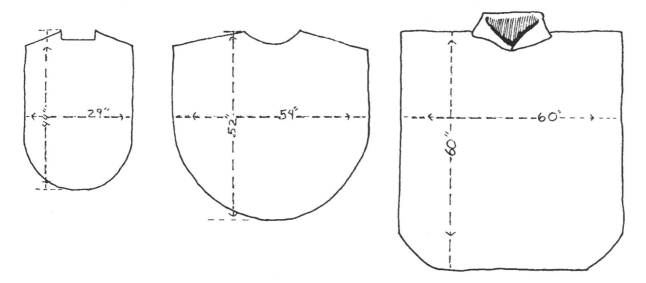

Figure 3-2. The standard chasuble sizes: small or Roman (29" x 44"), ample or Gothic (54" x 52") and large or monastic (60" x 60"). The necklines are interchangeable. Scale: ³⁄₁₆" equals 5".

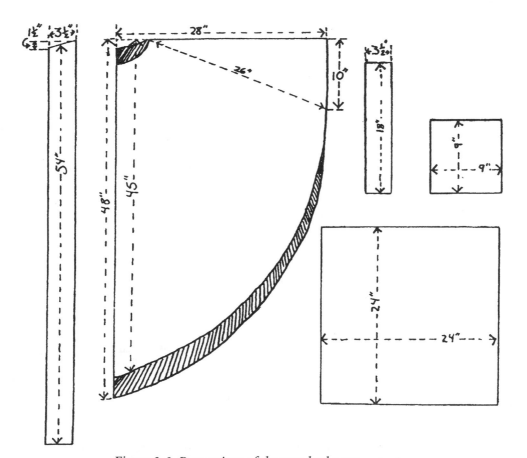

Figure 3-3. Proportions of the standard vestment set.
The stole and maniple are shown folded in half and the chasuble is quartered.
Scale: ³⁄₁₆" equals 2½". The pieces are from left to right and top to bottom: stole, chasuble, maniple, burse, chalice veil.

ornament will be seen when worn. The ornament on the chasuble, for instance, will be larger than one on the chalice veil. A stole designed to be worn on top of a chasuble may require ornaments of a different size than a stole worn underneath it.

The vestments are composed of particular shapes, originally civil pieces from Roman antiquity with nuances from the time of Jesus. Over time, the shapes have evolved from utilitarian to symbolic, and most people know little about the fundamental shapes and their meaning. However, education about the roots of the church's vestments helps enhance their liturgical use. Shape participates in liturgical *anamnesis*: it helps us remember the origins of the liturgy and its garments and it helps make the past present.

The codification of the vestment shapes poses a challenge to the maker who wants to avoid monotony and create interesting garments. Feasible modifications, such as adding a cowl collar or a V-neck, a fuller cut or tapering ends, lend some variation. The traditional size and shape of the vestments are standard, but the final size and style allow for interesting variations. The conventional chasuble sizes and shapes are: the Roman or stiffened, small-cut chasuble (around 29" by 44"); the Gothic, medium cut (around 54" by 52"); and the monastic or ample cut (around 60" by 60") (Figure 3-2). The primary rule to remember is to use the customary shape but allow right proportion to guide your final shape and style choice (Figure 3-3).[10]

Line and Ornament

Line is the essence of each piece. The line of the stole defines the role of the wearer. A diagonal slash line denotes a deacon; a crossed line, a priest; and a straight, bordered line, a bishop. Line creates a path that can vary in width, direction, length, curvature, and color. The seams where pieces of fabric join create lines, as do the applied trims. The lines created may indicate motion or stillness, fluidity or formality, joy or sorrow. Horizontal lines tend to be restful, while vertical lines aspire and diagonals agitate. Lines are used to suggest rhythm, variety, and balance. They may be long, flowing lines or short, chaotic lines; they may be thick or thin, wavy or jagged; they may be grouped formally, irregularly, or circuitously. The fabrics and trims stitched together create various lines that should be well proportioned and in harmony with the essential line of each article, bringing out the inner quality of each piece and the unity of the complete set.

Ornamentation is a way to play with line on the garments. When a chasuble is full and flowing, the fabric itself may be sufficient adornment. On the stoles, burse, veil, and a modest chasuble, embellishment may be more desirable. While never necessary, ornaments may be quite an effective design statement. Make the adornment an integral part of the design and not a mere accessory. Scant decorations that appear spotty are rarely successful. Adornment is a fine tool for adding emphasis and focus when it is harmoniously executed. Design a good scheme by noticing the lines and spaces created by and between the ornaments, and then mount them with care.

A number of terms are used to refer to the traditional ornaments used on vestments. They are defined below.

■ An APPAREL is an oblong, ornamental band of varying size and width. Usually embroidered, it adorns albs, amices, and sometimes tunics and altar frontals.

Figure 3-4.
An appareled alb.

Apparels originated during the thirteenth century as adornments of plain linen vestments for festival occasions. They consisted of embroidered geometric and/or symbolic figures worked into gold fabric or a corresponding chasuble fabric, or needleworked designs appropriate to the particular liturgical feast. During the nineteenth century, lace was a popular ornament on apparels. On the average, alb apparels measure fourteen by eight inches for the skirt and six by four inches for the sleeve (Figure 3-4). Sometimes an apparel simply refers to any narrow band of adornment used on vestments.

A variety of embroidered or appliquéd crosses are often worked at the ends of the stoles and maniple, in the center of the burse, and in the center of the front half of the chalice veil. The "kissing cross," so called because the minister kissed the cross before donning the garment, is the needleworked cross placed at the center back of the stole and center top of the maniple.

■ The FLOWER is the symbolic emblem attached at the center of the Y cross's fork.

■ GALLOONS are narrow bands used for bordering. Their actual width is determined in proportion to overall vestment size. Braids are common galloons and should be soft and supple. A stiff braid impedes the overall drape and creates wavy lines.

■ The LATIN CROSS (†) is a simple design, but it lacks fluidity and the horizontal arms tend to sag on the chasuble, unlike the Y cross. Since the Latin cross is replete with meaning, it may have stimulated the streamlined, stiffened Roman chasuble that could bear the Latin cross shape.

■ The ORPHREY is a three- to seven-inch wide embroidered or lace band. It hails from the *aurifrigium*, an embellishment of extreme elegance that took the place of the simple Roman *clavi* during the Middle Ages, and was originally used to conceal seams. When using the orphrey, consider the distance between the orphreys when determining their width. Notice the negative space (between and around the orphrey) and positive space (the actual orphrey) and place them to create effective lines (Figure 3-5).

Figure 3-5. The Y cross falling at the shoulder joint. The arms of the orphreys marked "A" are called "humerals" and the center pillar "B," a "dorsal." The center adornment is the "flower."

■ A PILLAR is the single straight band that extends the length of the chasuble. When placed on the front it is sometimes called a "pectoral," as opposed to the "dorsal" pillar on the back. They can be used to create a number of effects simply.

■ POWDERING and DIAPERING concern the overall pattern applied to the piece. Powdering is the repetition of separate, identical figures at regular intervals over the whole piece, while diapering is an overspreading design with connecting figuration (Figure 3-6).[11]

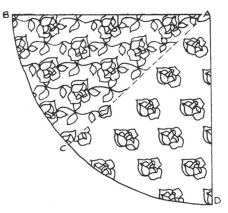

Figure 3-6. A directional pattern or nap requires that the material be cut and turned so that the front and back appear the same or upright. Lines A-B and A-D are the center folds; line A-C is the shoulder seam. A-B-C shows diapering, and A-C-D illustrates powdering.

■ The RATIONAL was a large, six-inch brooch used to fasten an open chasuble at the neck, embellishing an otherwise plain chasuble. It adorned the chasuble until the fourteenth century and may have been an imitation of the ancient Jewish rational.

■ A *VESICA* is a general term for any embroidered symbol used on vestments.

The Y cross is the earliest divergence from the straight band or pillar. It may have appeared to give a "home" to the flower within its fork; more likely, it appeared to mimic the lines of the ninth century *pallium* stole. The Y cross tends to be more pleasing than the straight Latin cross because it moves well with the chasuble. When it is placed exactly at the shoulder joint of the chasuble, the legs of the cross maintain their shape and do not slip downward (see Figure 3-5).

Ornamentation is the art of embellishing vestments with various designs, traditionally with appliqué or embroidery. Piecing is another effective way to create beautiful vestments. Many helpful products and sophisticated sewing machines help make these processes easy and exciting for the contemporary vestment maker. Adornments are successful when they have unity within the overall design, correct proportion to the size of the article, and a pleasing repetition, rhythm, and variety. A good rule of thumb is that a little ornamentation, well placed and well made, is sufficient. Choose shapes, dimensions, and textures that help the vestment fulfill its purpose and enhance the overall design. Ornamentation should emphasize the essential lines of the vestments without distracting from the unity of design.

Texture and Fabric

Texture has two dimensions, tactile and visual. We experience the tactile quality of the fabric as soft, nubby, stiff, or dense. Visual texture has more variety than tactile texture; we feel the fabric without actually touching it. We may feel with our hands that a raw silk is nubby, but we may see beyond its nubbiness to perceive a soft drape, high shine, and woven print. The assortment of fabrics we use can create a lush variety of texture or an austere simplicity. Each choice we make has unique patterns, light reflectivity, palpability, and drape. Moreover, a fabric's texture may be enhanced through stitchery, needlework, and trims. Texture is the maker's greatest ally, since the feel of the fabric can greatly influence the execution. The right fabric—well bodied, well textured, and richly colored—can prove irresistible. The joy we experience crafting it can permeate the completed piece. Love for the fabric, along with the pleasure of playing with its texture through stitchery and needlework, is what inspires many artists to work in textile projects.

The fabrics we choose for vestments will make or break the finished product. The materials should have a strong weave, a good hand (body), and appeal, but the choice of fabrics is abundant. No longer are we restricted to a rigorous protocol of acceptable fabrics, which was common during the 1800s. At that time the only fabrics in use were silk and velvet, brocade and satin, figured or plain. Silver and gold cloth were reserved for ornamentation; unbleached cotton was used for the lining. These materials continue to be excellent choices, but today many more fabrics are suitable, offering intriguing possibilities for vestment design. Luster, softness, body, and opacity are qualities to look for, yet skilled crafters can make exceptional use of muted, coarse, delicate, or sheer fabrics. Handwoven textiles feature the desired colors, texture, and figuration as part of the fabric. The warmth, textural interest, and flexibility of modern fabrics expands the possibilities for vestments into an almost limitless range of effects. Certain fabrics may be desirable for use in a particular climate or for the way they can stand up to tight storage and travel. Because the grade of fabric you choose will affect its appearance and performance, choose high quality fabrics for long-term durability. Look for consistent color, print, and grain throughout the yardage. More money spent at the outset may prove less costly in the long run.

Plain fabrics are always suitable when they have a good drape. Simple, unfigured fabrics are especially compatible with the themes of hope in Advent and penitence in Lent. Subtle figuration adds textural depth. Many samples in this book are made from fabrics that look solid at first glance, but on closer inspection reveal texture, which adds interest without being obtrusive. Overtly figured fabrics may be highly effective, but must be chosen with care so they don't look pretentious or unbecoming.

The body of the fabric affects the garment's drape. Limp, wispy fabrics do not convey the sense of quality needed for vesture; they appear weak and don't signal the important role vestments play in the worship service. Bulky materials are difficult to work with; they produce a stiff, frozen effect, and are too cumbersome and hot to wear. Pliant fabrics with a good drape can create a wealth of folds, making them a good choice for a chasuble, which is traditionally made from lightweight fabric. The chasuble moves easily with the minister, indicating a relaxed, welcoming mood.

One way to assure proper drape is to work with fabric that is on-grain. The grain of the fabric is the relationship of the warp (lengthwise) yarns and the fill (crosswise) yarns used to create woven cloth. The interlaced yarns should be at right angles to each other. If the yarns are skewed or bent, the drape will be skewed or bent. When selecting a fabric, check the grain. Be sure the warp runs parallel to the selvage edge. The fill can be checked by clipping then pulling a crosswise thread from the yardage, or by tearing the fabric crosswise. Neither the warp nor the fill should have more than a ⅜" variance from the selvage or torn edges. In addition, the grain differs in elasticity, which will affect the construction and drape. The lengthwise grain has minimal stretch, the crosswise grain gives a bit more, and the bias (45 degrees across both grains) has a good stretch. If a seam joins two different grain orientations, a crosswise and lengthwise, puckering and differential drape may result. If a chasuble is cut on the bias, the fabric should be allowed to hang for a few days to relax the stretch; otherwise, an uneven hemline will result. When checking the grain, pay attention to the relationship of the print to the grain. Whether or not the print is on-grain will be evident against the torn edge. Avoid an off-grain print—it will detract from the finished product.

A grain's texture affects the luminosity and color of the fabric. Some yardage is made with a balanced weave: the warp and fill have the same number of yarns per inch. They may be loosely or tightly woven. Luster is created by a satin weave in which the warp or fill skims over a number of yarns before interlacing. A satin weave or napped fabric (with a fuzzy surface such as velvet) will appear to be a different shade when its turned in a different direction. You may choose to use the shade change to create variety within a monochromatic (one-color) piece, but if you do not want the color change, be sure to have the weave/grain falling in the same direction when cut, then seamed (Figure 3-6).

A fabric's texture can draw our attention to the liturgical event and away from the many distractions of daily life we bring to worship. Just looking at a beautiful vestment can help us feel a quiet welcome to church. Too much texture, too much shine, and too much ornament, may, on the other hand, overwhelm or distract us. If a vestment is so striking that we focus on it rather than on the liturgy, it is not appropriate. Vestments are aesthetic pieces that point us in the right direction, rather than works of art designed to overpower the service. To achieve a successful results, the designer and the maker walk a fine line requiring skilled, modest reflection.

Color

Color plays an important role in forming our emotional response to worship. The abstemious "black and white" liturgies in the Anglican church of the eighteenth-century may have been prayerful, but they lacked the mood and depth of experience a liturgy couched in color achieves. Color can change the entire character of worship. Bold, bright colors will stimulate a more rousing response to the liturgy, while soft, muted tones will kindle a more subdued and soothing environment. Of course, the use of color is not absolute, but varies in accordance with the other elements of liturgy: the music, the proclamation of the Word, the prayers, and even the presider's appearance or mood. In addition, color is altered by its juxtaposition to other colors and to the light source. The carpet, the flowers, the time of day, and the candles will modify color endlessly. If shape is the enduring element of the vestments, color is the ephemeral ingredient. When choosing colors to use for the sanctuary, take fabric swatches into the worship space and observe them for a few weeks at varying times to see how the light and surrounding colors affect their appearance. Note whether the color comes alive or is dulled, invites or repels, harmonizes or agitates. A spectacular color in the store may prove lifeless in the sanctuary; an average color may come alive once placed in the church.

The importance of color in our psychological reactions has given color a wealth of symbolic meaning and has motivated liturgical color restrictions. These restrictions, described below, are helpful guidelines but are not definite rules. In using color for worship, follow the liturgical guidelines in conjunction with studying nature. Generally, nature provides large areas of restful colors accented with spots of brilliance. The liturgical color green, used for the longest season, is prolific in nature. Close scrutiny will reveal an infinite variety of greens accented by reds, blues, yellows, purples, and oranges. Color is an exciting and powerful design element that allows for freedom of expression, even within liturgical specifications.

A variety of approaches exists within the study of color theory, and there is no conclusive right or wrong way to use color. The traditional color wheel based on the primary colors of red, yellow, and blue helps us to identify how colors impact one another. Complementary colors are opposite each other on the wheel: red and green, orange and blue, yellow and violet (Figure 3-7). If mixed, these colors make gray, but when set side by side they intensify one another—they sing. Every pair of complements contains a warm and a cool color. Reds, oranges, and yellows are warm and stimulating because they are associated with the sun and fire; greens, blues, and violets are cool and soothing since they are identified with water and the forest.

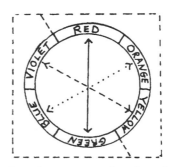

Figure 3-7. Complementary colors found on the color wheel: red and green, blue and orange, yellow and violet.

Analogous colors are next to each other on the wheel, making them harmonious. Analogous colors provide endless possibilities for the seemingly monochromatic liturgical colors. Yellow green highlights green, while blue green makes a stunning dark shadow; orange highlights red and purple is its shadow. Another way to combine colors is to use triads. Triads are composed of any three colors equidistant on the color wheel. Because the elements of the triad touch all areas of the color wheel, balance is emphasized. The primary colors of red, yellow, and blue form a triad. Our Trinitarian God resonates with the triadic balance; surely, God touches all areas of the spectrum of life. We use green for the season once called "Trinity" (now Pentecost). Perhaps a set of green

Figure 3-8. Two sets of triads: red, yellow, blue and violet, orange, green; and one tetrad: red violet, orange, yellow green, blue.

Figure 3-9. Two sets of split complements: red, yellow green, blue green; and yellow orange, blue, violet.

vestments accented with orange and violet would seize our Trinitarian sensibilities. A tetrad consists of four colors equidistant on the wheel and may be identified using the points of a square placed within the color wheel. The four colors will create a harmonious quartet; for example, yellow, blue green, violet, and red orange (Figure 3-8). Finally, split complementaries provide a common alliance of colors. A color is selected and then, instead of using its opposite, the two colors flanking its complement are used. Red, blue green, and yellow green; or blue, yellow orange, and red orange are split complements (Figure 3-9).

Use the dynamics of color to experiment with the liturgical colors and how they might produce provocative effects in the worship space. The dynamics will vary when set against white, the foundational liturgical color. Gold is a variation of yellow with its own dynamics. An iridescent fabric that reflects the full or rainbow spectrum of light offers another variation, as do lustrous or sheer fabrics. Play and experiment. The choices are far greater than the classic five liturgical colors.

The Liturgical Colors

The practice of using vestments to systematically mark the liturgical seasons came relatively late. The ancient vestments were made from the white, undyed linen of the typical tunic. White was simple, modest, and festive.

It was the only significant liturgical color. The clergy steered away from the extravagant and stately scarlets, purples, and golds of the Roman nobility. Clement of Alexandria (circa 150–210) encouraged the use of white because, as Psalm 51:7 suggests, it is pure and uncontaminated: "[W]ash me, and I shall be whiter than snow." As the social status of the church grew, the clergy adopted rich color and fine fabrics. When the use of color became excessive, the church councils responded with constraint. The 589 Council at Narbonne, for example, forbade the use of barbaric purple; and in 787, the Second Council at Nicaea prohibited the flagrant use of rich and brilliant colors.[12]

With the rise of the monastic movement, black dress predominated. Clerics dressed in a dark color to symbolize a life of penitence, devotion, and holiness. The monk's habit was normally dark, and clergy into the twenty-first century continue to wear black. As a general rule of thumb, traditionally the clergy wore black in public and to preach, and white to administer the sacraments, except in England, where red was the liturgical color of choice.

In spite of counsel to the contrary, clergy continued to wear a variety of colors while presiding at the liturgy and at large. While black remained the color for civil wear, Pope Innocent III (1198–1216) commended the use of four liturgical colors for Roman Catholic clergy: white for the high feast days and for the seasons from Christmas to Epiphany and Easter to Pentecost; red for Pentecost and for the feasts of the martyrs; black for the penitential seasons of Advent and Lent and a few other specific days; and green for the ferial (ordinary) days and seasons. Modifications were made with the addition of violet in 1286 to replace black except on Good Friday and at masses for the dead. By 1570, the five-color scheme (white, red, violet, black, and green) was adopted; few revisions followed. Before the Oxford movement, Anglicans wore the reformed black-and-white ensemble of cassock, surplice, hood, and tippet, but the Anglican Anglo-Catholic revival of the 1800s eventually spread the Roman scheme into the Protestant sphere.

The five-color scheme has remained the norm for the past six hundred years, but it has never achieved homogeneity. Variations are found regionally due to taste and financial resources. Blue has often been affiliated with the feasts of the Virgin, especially during the Middle Ages; yellow has been used for Lent; and a combination of colors is common for All Saints' Day, November 1. In the East, white is used except during the penitential seasons, when dark colors are used. Colors also vary for particular services independent of the season. White is used for weddings, baptisms, and funerals (formerly black), and violet for confessions.

In the 1960s, the Vatican II council set a revised standard color scheme to punctuate the cycle of the liturgical seasons. Since that time the system has been followed by the liturgical churches in the West. Colors include: blue or purple for Advent; white from Christmas through Epiphany and Easter until Pentecost, on other major feast days, and for the burial of the dead; red on Pentecost, Palm Sunday, Good Friday, the feasts of the martyrs, and for ordinations; purple for the penitential season of Lent and a few other specific days; and green for the ferial days and seasons. Rose is optional for use on the Third Sunday of Advent and the Fourth Sunday in Lent. Black is rarely used in liturgy other than for penitential adornment.

A standard color code does not prevail: a variety of colors, alone and combined, make up contemporary vestments. Distinctive colors complement the rhythm of the liturgical calendar. Vestments are a part of an aesthetic whole that creates a framework conducive for worship throughout the year. Clear, compatible, and harmonious colors germane to the season and to the overall environment enhance and express the liturgical mood. The primary liturgical colors and their symbolism follow, in alphabetical order.

- Black emulates civil mourning dress in ancient Rome. From the Middle Ages until the 1960s, black was used on Good Friday and for funerals. The recent liturgical renewal called for a return to the white of the ancient church. Black is the hue of sorrow and marks loss, penance, and the day of the crucifixion.
- Blue is the color associated with the Virgin Mary, since it is associated with truth, constancy, fidelity, and heaven. Blue is occasionally used as a variation of violet for feasts of the Virgin and of saints who are confessors rather than martyrs. White replaced the use of blue in the sixteenth century. Blue continued to be used in the Sarum rites to represent the Virgin and the expanse of God's love. It has found its way back into the liturgical spectrum for use during Advent. Blue is used to distinguish the hopeful expectation of Advent as distinct from the penitential purple of Lent.
- Gold may be used in place of all colors except black and violet. Most commonly, gold is the preferred color for ornamentation, unless black is the dominant color. On black vestments, silver or white ornamentation is substituted. Gold is used to symbolize purity, divinity, and kingship in accord with its inherent value, its civil use, and its history as one of the gifts offered to Jesus by the Magi.

- Green dominates most of the liturgical year; it is used during ordinary time, and the seasons of Epiphany and Pentecost. Green, the prevailing color of nature, represents growth, the hope of spring, new life, and immortality.
- Gray, the color of ashes, signifies mourning, humility, and the innocent accused. It is especially appropriate as a Lenten accent.
- Purple, more red than blue violet, is the color of royalty and power because purple dye was held in high esteem by ancient peoples. The dye was highly stable and a lush color, making it very valuable. When Alexander the Great conquered Susa, he claimed 280,000 tons of Hermione purple, a cache of incredible wealth. Lydia, the woman of faith in Acts, is thought to have been wealthy because she dealt in purple cloth (Acts 16:14). Purple is also associated with penitence, because it is made by mixing red (passion) and blue (devotion) into a reddish violet. It may be used during Advent and Lent and on Rogation days, Ember days, and for vigils.
- Red symbolizes fire, blood, divine love, the Holy Spirit, and God's creative power. At Pentecost and ordinations it symbolizes the descent of Holy Spirit in the form of tongues of fire on the assembled apostles (Acts 2:3). Red is worn on Palm Sunday, during Holy Week, and for the commemoration of the Holy Innocents and martyrs, to symbolize the shedding of Christ's blood and that of his followers.
- Rose, the color of dawn's early light, calls forth rejoicing because the sun (Son) comes soon and the end is near. It is used for the Third (*Gaudete*) Sunday of Advent and the Fourth (*Laetare*) Sunday in Lent to signal the midpoint of each season.
- Silver is an alternative to white.
- Violet draws its significance from the flower of the same name and hue. The low-growing violet is prized for its humility, and this color symbolizes the humility of God, who became human through Jesus. Because its purplish-blue hue represents suffering, penitence, and humility, it is the preferred color for the penitential season of Lent.
- White is the color of purity in psalms, and was the color of joy and festivity in ancient Rome. In addition, it symbolizes innocence, holiness, and the Virgin Mary. White evokes a mood of celebration and rejoicing; it is used for all high feast days, days devoted to the Virgin, and at funerals to mark the gateway into eternal life.
- Yellow, when pure, represents faith, divinity, the sun, and God's goodness. When dingy it signifies jealousy and deceit, especially that of Judas. Yellow

should be used with care as an accent to the other liturgical colors.

Some color combinations have developed additional significance. Popular black and white represent purity with penance and humility. Blue and red denote heavenly truth and love. Red and white signify love and wisdom or innocence. Red and black denote the devil and hell.

STYLE

You can create vestments that maintain continuity with the historic church while simultaneously reflecting your personal taste. The imprint of your personal style comes through in your choice of fabric and pattern, the quality of your construction, and your final presentation. Your artistic expression is influenced by what has been made before, the specific worship environment, the materials available, and your own inspiration. You carry elements into your work that cannot be explained. They are the gifts you bring to the craft. You may rely on the principles and elements of design, the tradition of the church, prayer, and skilled training—all of these and more account for the quality of your vestments. But it is your personal imprint that makes each handmade vestment a gift rather than a product of a manufacturer. Commercial vestments may be handsome, but they can never produce the life and beauty embodied in gifts of the people.

NOTES

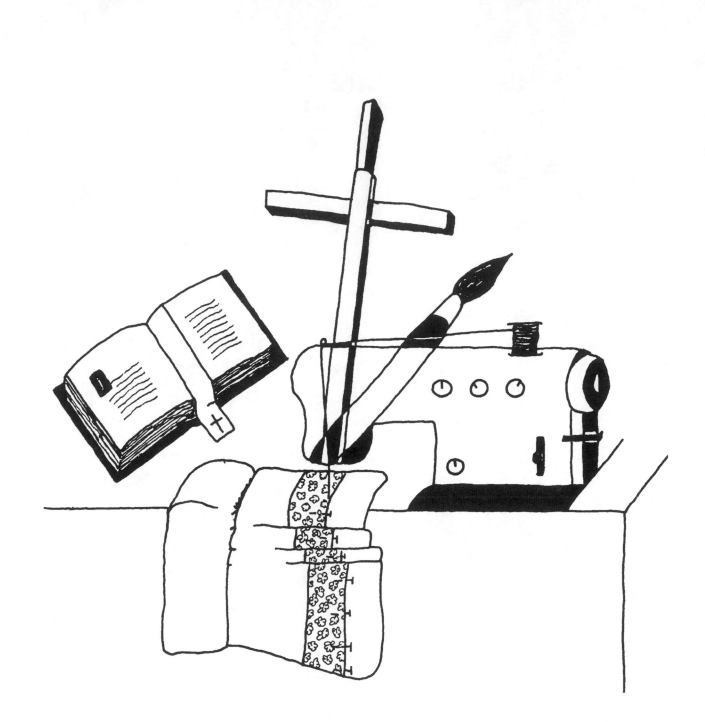

4.
STITCHING IN THE SPIRIT

Let the [work of my hands] and the meditation of my heart be acceptable to you, O Lord, my rock and my redeemer.

—Psalm 19:14 (rephrased)

We are called to worship God "in spirit and truth." One approach to God and the spiritual life is through symbols. Vestments are symbols: they are external garments used for approaching the holy. Over the years, particular meaning has been attached to vestments in order to identify their spiritual meaning. Some of the ways that Eucharistic attire has been interpreted follow. Beyond symbolism, the art of creating vestments opens us to God and enriches the worship of the community. This chapter explores the spirituality we associate with vestments through symbol, personal devotion, and corporate blessing.

ON SYMBOLISM

Vestments are imbued with meaning. They are visible reminders of our continuity with the early church and of the special role of ministers within the church. With vestments, the past is made present as the worshiping community engages in the Eucharistic event.

In the West there are two lines of thought regarding the mystical meaning of vestments. One idea holds that vestments represent the bonds of Christ, the robes of mockery, or has other associations with the Passion, suffusing the articles with meaning.

- The amice is the veil with which Christ's eyes were bound during his mockery.
- The alb is the linen in which Joseph of Arimathea arrayed the crucified Christ.
- The girdle is the cord of the scourging.

- The stole symbolizes the ropes by which Christ was bound to the pillar for torture.
- The maniple represents the bonds that fastened Christ's hands.
- The chasuble is the purple robe that Pontius Pilate conferred on Christ.
- The second line of thought reminds the minister of the Christian graces and virtues associated with the clerical role. This tradition is looser and lacks a central thesis. The prayers in chapter two that correlate with the individual vestments derive from this strain.
- The amice represents faith. Because it is the first item laid on the head, it is the helmet of salvation. It also symbolizes moderation of speech, since it covers the neck from whence the voice proceeds.
- The alb symbolizes purity or redemption.
- The girdle represents chastity, modesty, and/or integrity.
- The stole represents humility because it is worn like a yoke and forms a cross when crossed over the breast or the shoulder. It is also the robe of immortality given in Baptism.
- The maniple represents fortitude since it resembles a sword; also zeal and suffering and/or penitence and servitude.
- The chasuble symbolizes the charity that covers all, the sweet yoke of Christ and/or the burden of the priest's responsibility and obedience.
- The dalmatic and tunicle symbolize the robe of justice.

Eastern Christians attach other symbolic values to the vestments:

- The *vakas* (amice) is a sign of obedience to Christ and of the yoke of Christ.
- The *shabik* (alb/*stoicharion*) is a sign of purity and gladness of heart.
- The *kodee* (girdle) is a sign of faith, spiritual strength, and the priestly authority to bind and loose.
- The *phorourar* (stole/*epitrachelion*) signifies the Christian duty of righteousness.
- The *bazpan* (maniple or cuff/*epigonation*) is a sign of cleanliness and the fortitude to serve Christ.
- The *shoorchar* (chasuble/*phelonion*) signifies faith, the glory of the spiritual life, and the shield that defends against evil.

Out of personal piety, we can give too much weight to the symbolism of vestments. Symbolism is best held lightly and adhered to only if it helps to focus our minds on worship. More than just utilitarian accoutrements of worship, vestments provide a visual cue to "remember" and they enrich the focus of the communal gathering. The symbolism associated with vestments during the Middle Ages was construed when "symbol giving" was prevalent in order to deepen and enrich worship. Vestments do not need symbolic meaning or decorative symbols to serve their purpose. Simplicity, proportion, and unity will generate garments of beauty and enhance the liturgy.

Decorative symbols are most effective when they are integral parts of the design. Use them sparingly and simply. Open, empty space is like the silence that allows us to hear the still small voice. Vestments are not commercial or educational tools; therefore, symbols on these garments are not appropriate sources of information. When you choose symbols to adorn vestments, remember that vestments should call "Come unto me" and not be "heavy laden." Good design sense, scriptural meditation, and sound research will help you use symbols effectively. Three books on symbols I find indispensable are: *The Dictionary of Christian Lore and Legend* by J. C. J Metford (London: Thames and Hudson, 1983); *Saints, Signs and Symbols by W. Ellwood Post* (Harrisburg, Pa.: Morehouse Publishing, 1974); and *A Dictionary of Symbols* by J. E. Cirlot (New York: Philosophical Library, 1971).

The primary symbols associated with the liturgical seasons include, but are not limited to:

- Advent—Advent wreath with four candles, the *alpha* and *omega*, the Jesse tree.
- Christmas—manger, angel, sheep and shepherds, Christmas rose, light, Christmas tree, holly, IHS.
- Epiphany—Magi or crowns, star, gifts (especially gold, frankincense, and myrrh).
- Lent—ashes, raven, dragon, lamb.
- Holy Week—palms, cross or crucifix, crown of thorns, whips, and other instruments of the Passion.
- Easter—butterfly, lily, egg, ivy, lamb with a cross-emblazoned banner, paschal candle, pomegranate.
- Pentecost—dove, seven tongues of fire, seven doves.
- Trinity—equilateral triangle, "holy, holy, holy," three interwoven circles.

SEWING ROOM SPIRITUALITY

Working from the heart and in a spirit of humility, the vestment maker can move beyond mere craft to experience vestment making on a deeper level. It can become prayer.

Prayer is an inner response to God, an invitation to know God. Vestment making as prayer begins with the discovery that our creativity is a response to God's call. Love of the needle, the liturgy, and, most especially, of God, sustains our work from its preparation and creation to its final presentation. The preceding chapter addressed the elements of design used to promote beautiful vestments. Spirituality is an inarticulate element of design expressed through personal style; it is an essential component that weaves the Spirit into the garments.

Prayer can be done in many different ways. It includes all of our thoughts, deeds, designing, and sewing when they are a response to God. The traditional types of prayer include meditation, oblation, adoration, praise, petition and intercession, thanksgiving, and penitence. Each of these prayer forms may be used simultaneously or separately as your vestment project proceeds. Allow yourself to experience the many levels and types of prayer that God calls forth. Your prayerful response will guide your work and will be manifest in your final product.

Meditation involves listening intentionally to God. The practice calls us to set aside distractions and to be fully present to God, abandoned to the promptings of the Spirit. The routine of the craft, worship, *lectio divina*, and journaling are excellent opportunities that help us set aside preconceived notions and open ourselves to God. This openness fosters in us an attitude of "pilgrim maker"; we become ready to give ourselves entirely to the community and to God through the art of the needle. Listening before the inception of your design may open new avenues of expression deeply grounded in the community and in the Spirit.

Worshipping with the community that commissioned the vestment can be an invaluable source of inspiration. By focusing on the physical setting, smells, sights, and colors of the church, you can find inspiration for reflecting the community's unique spirit in the garment. Knowing the priest who will wear the vestment as well as the laity he presides over is equally important. Abandon yourself to the worship, listen to the community, and allow the Spirit to speak.

Lectio divina, an ancient monastic tradition, promotes an awareness of God's presence through a fourfold process of sacred reading. Choose your readings from the Scriptures and prayers germane to the liturgical season. To begin, read the selected text slowly and intentionally. Continue to read the text in this manner two or three times and allow it to sink in. You may center on a single word, on a phrase that stands out, or on the complete text. Second, meditate on the text by allowing it to stir your imagination; be fully present to what arises. Third, yield to prayer in whatever way is called forth. Fourth, sit in contemplation by being still and basking in the presence of God. Close your meditation with a prayer of thanksgiving for the time spent with God and God's Word.[13]

Following worship and *lectio*, record your thoughts or images in a journal or sketchbook. Use the time of journaling and sketching to reflect and play with words and images from the Scriptures, prayers, worship environment, liturgical colors and symbols, and the patterns in this book. The impressions that emerge may give some surprising direction to your project and provide invaluable aid to your selection of fabrics, patterns, and methods of construction.

After the design of your vestments is set, you are ready to begin production, which calls for skill. The pattern drafting, cutting, and stitching require careful, concentrated effort. Yet there is a transcendent quality to the making: the repetitive measuring, cutting, and stitching provide an absorbing form of meditative prayer. The most important thing you can put into your work is yourself, with all of your skills and shortcomings. When the self is stitched into the project through love, the self becomes a part of the *gestalt* of the making; the whole becomes greater than the parts combined. The traditional forms of prayer are wonderful supports for making your work into an offering of your heart to the community and to God. Begin your work sessions with an oblation, a self-surrender or giving of yourself fully to God. Pray:

All that I am and all that I have is yours, O Lord.
Use me to bear your light and love in this holy work.

Follow with adoration, which declares your profound love of God and desire to work for God, empty of self-serving desires, ambitions, and needs. Pray:

Empty my thoughts of all things worldly,
O Lord, and inspire me with your love.
Empty my hands of all insincere craft,
O Lord, and fill them with skill for love of you.
Empty my soul of all vainglory, O Lord,
and fill me with love of you for your glory.

Sit quietly for a moment to bask in God's love. It may help to imagine being cradled in Christ's loving arms. Conclude your opening prayers of oblation and adoration with a petition for your work and with praise, the celebration of God and God's passionate and abundant love for us. Pray:

O God of truth and beauty,
prosper the work of my hands.
Teach me to see in you the source of my talent
and help me to offer it for
the adornment of worship of you.
My heart and hands are ready and
filled with praise of you, O Lord.
For yours is the honor and glory
now and for ever. Amen.[14]

In addition to the absorption of the craft, a less formal way to pray that naturally weaves itself into your work is colloquy, or conversation. It is a wonderful way to be in constant dialogue with God as you progress through your project. A popular example of colloquy comes from Teresa of Avila (1515–1582). When she fell into a creek after a hard day, she shouted, "After everything else, now this!"

"That's how I treat my friends," responded God, her constant companion.

"Then no wonder you have so few!" cried the enraged saint. This lively form of prayer helps to keep contact with God in the forefront of our thoughts: right here, right now. Praise, intercession, thanksgiving, and penitence are all avenues for colloquy. When a difficult seam turns out just right, you might exclaim meaningfully, "Praise the Lord!" or "Thank you, God."

Petition for yourself and intercession for others appeal for the "kingdom come on earth as it is in heaven." Arrow prayers are short intercessory prayers that address a specific need as the need arises. For example: "Lord, I feel incapable of this task, guide my hands that I may do it right," or "Bless all those who helped to make this beautiful piece of cloth, from the farmers to the manufacturers to the clerk who sold it to me at the store." Or, "For the impoverished churches, may they, too, have someone to provide vestments to enhance their worship," or "For those who have given generously to the Body but because of age or illness can no longer exercise their talents." As you create with your hands, be creative in your prayer life so that your prayer and your project may be stitched together in love.

Penitence seeks reconciliation with God and others when we have erred or strayed. It names where we have "missed the mark," accepts responsibility for our part, and looks for ways to change in order to align ourselves more closely to God's will. How we work with others in preparation for and execution of our project may be an area of penitence—of reconnecting with God and with those we may have hurt along the way. Inviting someone who may feel isolated to help with the handwork may be a form of reconciliation. Or penitence may help you over the hump of an apparently irreparable mistake made while working on the project. I had forgotten to double the lengths when cutting the sections for the Lenten chasuble, dalmatic, and tunicle (chapter 9) from a beloved handwoven fabric that had been given to me by a dear friend. When I realized that I had erroneously cut up the beautiful cloth, I sobbed for God's and my friend's forgiveness for ruining the project. Exhausted by tears, I knelt to meditate, to pray, to listen. A mantra (a short, repetitious prayer) came, imperceptibly at first, then more strongly as it permeated my being: "out of ashes, O Lord." The mantra gradually reconciled me with my error and strengthened me to go on. The work of piecing was grueling, since I knew it should have been a simple, seamless project. The love and hope discovered through reconciliation allowed me to work tirelessly and to see the project to its completion instead of stuffing the whole mess into a closet. "May those who [sew] in tears reap with shouts of joy" (Psalm 126:5).

Blessing the Vestments

Creating any art, including vestments, is about waiting patiently for the unseen to be revealed, working toward it in hope and perseverance, thanksgiving and self-surrender, sometimes blunderingly so, until that great moment when the project is completed. Then you, the artist, are called to give your creation to the community. It's appropriate for the worshiping community to bless the vestments as an act of acceptance and thanksgiving. The event may be simple; it's an excellent time to describe the garments' history, use,

and symbolism. On the first day the vestments are used, lay them out in plain view of the people—a table in the midst of the congregation works well. Have the minister(s) enter unvested or in alb(s). The structure of the blessing may proceed as follows:

1. A brief introduction.
2. Silence.
3. Invite the people to pray.
4. Bless the article and the wearer that they may take on the mind of Christ and perform the service in accord with the designated vestment (see blessings below).
5. Sprinkle with holy water or use incense (optional).
6. The minister(s) don the vestment(s).
7. Conclude with a thanksgiving.

Normally, the extra pieces such as the chalice veil, burse, and maniple are not blessed individually, but are given a general blessing with the chasuble to which they are attached. Some suggested blessings follow:

Blessing for Priest's and/or Bishop's Stole and Chasuble

Holy and gracious God, we ask your blessing upon this stole [and chasuble]. We set these garments aside for bishops and priests as they preside at the Holy Eucharist. May their presiding be like the servant leadership of Jesus Christ, who came to serve and not to be served. May your bishops and priests proclaim your Word with grace, vigor, and courage; may they preside at the Eucharist with humility, reverence, and awe. May their lives reflect their ministry. Now bless, +, this stole [and chasuble]: In the Name of the Father [Creator], and of the Son [Holy Word] and of the Holy Spirit. Amen.

Blessing for Deacon's Stole and/or Dalmatic

Holy and gracious God, we ask your blessing upon this stole [and dalmatic]. We set these garments aside for your deacons to wear in the proclamation of your holy Gospel, prayers of intercession for the church and for the world, and the administration of your Sacrament. May the deacons who wear these garments have the mind of Christ Jesus: a servant ministry of bringing the church to the world and the world to the church. Bless, +, this stole as a symbol of the ordained ministry of service and proclamation: may the deacons who wear it live the Gospel they proclaim. Bless, +, this dalmatic and those who wear it as a sign of worship, leadership, and reverence. Amen.

Blessing for Lay Minister's Tunicle

Holy and gracious God, we ask your blessing upon this tunicle. We set this garment aside for your ministers to wear for the proclamation of your Word and the administration of your Sacrament. May the ministers who wear this tunicle have the mind of Christ Jesus, who came to serve and not to be served. May the ministers proclaim your Word with reverence and potency and administer the Holy Communion with humility and grace. May their lives reflect this ministry.

We ask this blessing, +, in the Name of the Father [Creator], and of the Son [Holy Word], and of the Holy Spirit. Amen.

A General Blessing

Gracious and bountiful God, we beseech you to bless, +, by the power of the Holy Spirit, this [name the article] made ready for divine worship. May your grace and loving-kindness descend on all who are to use it, so that they may reflect your holiness and presence in themselves and to those whom they minister. May they be aided by your mercy; through Christ our Lord. Amen.

5.
GENERAL INSTRUCTIONS

They maintain the fabric of the world, and their concern is for the exercise of their trade.

—Sirach 38:34

Before you begin your project, review the fundamental information in this chapter to help you complete the pattern instructions that follow. Provided are: a general supply list; several basic guidelines; a key to the illustrations; some basic stitches and finishes; instructions for attaching interfacing, making bias strips, preparing binding and constructing cording; methods for enlarging the patterns; the general instructions for assembling the different vestment pieces; and a vestment planning sheet.

GENERAL SUPPLIES

Here is a list of basic supplies you will need for the sewing projects included in this book:

1. Scissors: sharp dressmaker shears (good scissors are important) and a small pair for fine and trim work.
2. Pins: use fine long silk pins to avoid snags or holes caused by standard pins (glass-head fine pins are good).
3. Thread to match the color and type of fabric. Use a natural (cotton) thread for natural fibers and synthetic thread with synthetic fabrics. Use a good-quality thread. Avoid threads that appear fuzzy on the spool, because they will break and cause havoc to your sewing machine. Mettler's highly mercerized "silk"-finished cotton is a good bet.
4. Pattern tracing fabric or paper (ironed) for drafting the patterns.
5. Removable fabric marker: test the marker on a scrap of fabric to be sure it is removable since the marker may behave differently from one fabric to the next. Ask a knowledgeable fabric salesperson to recommend a suitable marker for your project. Usually a soft lead pencil works the best. Avoid pens with disappearing or wash-out ink—they often "ghost" or come back, especially when set with a steam iron.
6. Point turner for turning out neat corners and creasing seams.
7. Measuring tools: 48" straight edge; clear, gridded 24" and 6" rulers; a tape measure.
8. Styling design ruler for drafting accurate curves.
9. Machine needles: excellent quality machine needles appropriate to the task at hand. Schmetz makes suitable needles and clearly states their purpose on each package (sewing, quilting, or embroidery). Most sewing machine problems are due to poor quality, inappropriate, or old needles. Use good needles and change them often.
10. Hand needles: an assortment of sharps for general hand sewing and appliqué; betweens if you plan to hand quilt the quilted rose or green chasuble; embroidery needles.
11. Worktable: a 4' x 6' sheet of plywood covered with sheet plastic or other smooth, resilient surface. Set the plywood at your correct working height to avoid back strain. An assortment of supports may be used from bureaus to sawhorses. A large, steady table is worth its weight in gold. It allows you to spread your work out flat for measuring, cutting, pinning, and hand stitching. Be sure the table is clean and smooth. If you are serious about

vestment making, purchase a 40" by 72" gridded mat (available from Sew/Fit Company, 1-800-547-4739).

12. Books are invaluable for clarifying basic sewing questions and inspiring your own creativity. *The Quilter's Ultimate Visual Guide from A-Z*, edited by Ellen Pahl (Emmaus, Pa.: Rodale Press, 1997), is an excellent resource. A basic sewing book such as *The Vogue Sewing Book* or the *Complete Guide to Sewing* from Reader's Digest would also be helpful, along with a basic book for embroidery stitches.

Optional but helpful items available at most quilt shops include:

1. A walking foot with a ¼" and a ½" guide to assure smooth seams and quilting.
2. An appliqué foot if you plan to machine appliqué.
3. Fray Block™ by June Tailor dries soft and prevents fraying in spots that might otherwise be problematic.
4. Basting adhesive to hold difficult areas while stitching, especially the burse.
5. A rotary cutter, straight edge, and special "self-healing" cutting mat for ease of cutting straight and accurately.
6. Fabric weights instead of pins to hold the pattern in place.
7. Long and slender flower head pins for lining up pieced fabric.

SOME BASIC GUIDELINES

Since human bodies differ in size and shape, alterations are inevitable. Make muslin samples first to check fit, particularly the deacon's stoles.

Read all the instructions through completely before beginning a project to get a sense of the whole project. Some steps in the process may not make much sense unless you know what steps come later. But remember, they will make far more sense once you have the fabric in hand.

Preshrink fabric if you plan to wash the vestments after they are made up, although dry cleaning is usually better in order to maintain the fabric's color and body.

Cut accurately.

Remember to transfer all markings to the fabric before removing the pattern.

Reserve pattern pieces since you may be using them more than once.

Baste and stitch carefully with correct needle and thread to avoid puckers and unsightly seams. Remember not to skip steps; if you do, your garment might not look well constructed in the end.

If the fabric width needs to be pieced, try to place the seam where an orphrey or other adornment will conceal the seam. Remember to add seam allowances to both pieces.

Allow for extra yardage if you are using a figured material that requires matching.

With a napped or patterned fabric, take care to turn the fabric so that both sides of the vestment have the same nap or the pattern matches down both halves. Check for nap before cutting. If a nap exists, cut and turn one side of the fabric 180 degrees, then seam it back together. If the pattern does not call for a seam, be sure to add a seam allowance before you cut.

Finish all raw edges: serge, if possible, or use one of the following methods: machine zigzag along the edge; turn the edge under ¼" and stitch with a straight stitch; stitch ¼" from the raw edge and pink with pinking shears; or oversew the raw edge by hand.

Press all seams open unless serged or if the directions state otherwise. Clip where necessary to press seams flat. Snip tight selvage edges, if retained, to avoid puckering.

Iron wisely and with care. You will be working with fine fabrics that may shrink, distort, or scorch when ironed at high temperatures. Always test a fabric scrap for steam tolerance and heat sensitivity. Normally, steam is the best choice to give a firm, smooth finish. Some fabrics need to be protected with a press cloth when you iron them.

The lining of the vestment need not be a liturgical color, and can be used to add contrast to the vestment. Its weight should complement the main fabric and it should slip easily over the alb. Satin is always a good choice. Avoid using fabrics that may sag.

Interface the stoles but not the chasuble, unless a sheer is being used and the interlining provides body that the outer fabric lacks. Hobbs "Thermore" or preshrunk flannelette are good choices when a chasuble interlining is called for. Avoid fusible interfacing—it tends to cause puckers and an uneven quality to the fabric. The sew-in variety is worth the small extra effort.

The seam allowance is ½" unless otherwise stated.

Lay dust sheets over your project when you are not working on it, especially if you have a cat who likes to sit on your fabric.

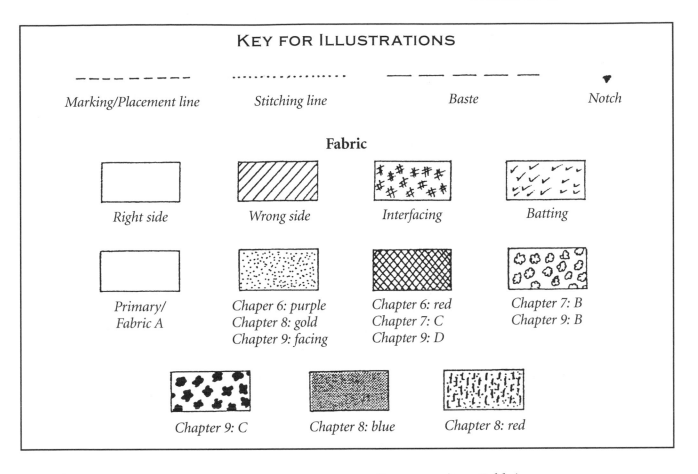

KEY FOR ILLUSTRATIONS

Marking/Placement line   *Stitching line*   *Baste*   *Notch*

Fabric

Right side   *Wrong side*   *Interfacing*   *Batting*

Primary/
Fabric A

Chaper 6: purple
Chapter 8: gold
Chapter 9: facing

Chapter 6: red
Chapter 7: C
Chapter 9: D

Chapter 7: B
Chapter 9: B

Chapter 9: C   *Chapter 8: blue*   *Chapter 8: red*

STITCHES AND FINISHES

You need to know the following basic stitches and finishes to construct the patterns in chapters 6–11.

Basting stitch: Weave the needle in the same manner as the running stitch, only use long, ¼" to ½" stitches.

Blind appliqué or slip stitch: Run the needle through the fold of the top fabric, bring the needle out at the folded edge to catch a few yarns of the bottom (garment) fabric, insert needle back into the folded edge close to where you exited. For appliqué, give the needle a slight tug when you exit the fold to completely hide the previous stitch under the folded edge.

Ease stitch: Use a hand-running or a machine-basting stitch just inside the seam line or hem fold on the longer fabric that needs to be eased (for example, the curved edge of a hem). Pull up the thread and distribute the fullness evenly as you pin to fit the shorter fabric.

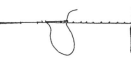

Corners, mitre: Fold in hem allowance on all edges and crease with your fingers or the iron. Then open out the corners and fold the corner in along the intersection of the crease lines. Refold the hem allowance to form the mitre, as shown.

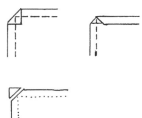

Turn: To reduce the bulk before turning a corner, trim off the seam allowance at an angle just beyond the stitching. Use a point turner to sharpen the turn.

Running or quilt stitch: Weave the point of the needle in and out of the fabric layers a few times before pulling the thread through. Keep the stitches and the spaces between the stitches small and even, around eight to ten stitches per inch. When quilting, it may be easier to work toward your body and keep one hand on the underside of the fabrics.

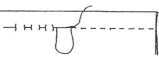

Stay stitch: Always stay stitch the neck edges of the vestments for an even, stable neckline. Just inside the seam line, machine stitch through a single thickness toward the center of the garment unless you cut a V neck, in which case, stitch from the center of  the V toward the shoulder. A loosely woven fabric should be stay stitched on all the cut edges.

Trim, grade, and clip seams:

1. Trim the seam allowance to slightly more than half its width.
2. Trim one layer of the seam allowance a bit more.
3. On a curved seam, clip periodically into the seam allowance, stopping just short of the stitching. This allows for smooth seams

Understitch: After clipping and grading a seam, press the facing open, then stitch the facing to the seam allowance close to the seam line, keeping the garment free from the facing. 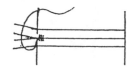 This prevents the facing from rolling toward the garment's right side.

Whipstitch: Insert the needle into the seam allowance of the first fabric and bring it up through the second, whip the needle back to insert close to the first insertion and bring it out close to the first exit. Continue for about ¼". Use the whipstitch to reinforce stitching and to join the burse sections. To apply ribbon, "whip" the needle through both layers using close, even stitches the entire length of the edge to be worked.

PREPARATION BASICS

General Instructions for Attaching Interfacing

1. For facings, baste interfacing to the wrong side of fabric, just inside the seam line. Trim the interfacing close to the basting. The interfacing should just catch into the seam stitch without excess.
2. For stoles, align the interfacing (cut to the exact finished stole size) to the seam line on the wrong side of the fabric. Baste, then catch stitch in place (see Figure 9-DT2, page 109). Remove the basting.

Making Bias Strips

1. To make specific projects on the bias, look in the applicable chapter for yardage. However, if you

need to estimate the size of a fabric square to yield the necessary number of bias strips, use this formula: first, multiply the desired strip width times the total length needed; then, using a calculator, find the square root of the total, round to the nearest inch, and add a few inches. Your answer tells you how big to cut the fabric square. Example: 2" width x 360" (10 yards) = 720"; $\sqrt{720}$ = 26.8, round up to 27", + 3" = 30" square needed—use a 36" square for fewer joining seams.

2. Draw a diagonal line from one corner to the opposing corner on fabric cut square to the grain. Draw lines parallel to the first line at intervals equivalent to the desired strip width (Figure 5-BS2). Cut the fabric along drawn lines (a rotary cutter is ideal for this task).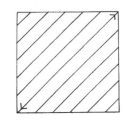

Figure 5-BS2.
The cutting of bias strips from a fabric square.

3. Stack the strips with all the right sides up. The 45 degree angles at the ends should all angle in the same direction. Correct any ends that are not properly oriented.

4. With right sides together, place two ends together, offset ¼" (Figure 5-BS4). Pin and stitch in a ¼" seam. Press seam open and trim excess seam allowance. Continue adding strips until the desired length is achieved.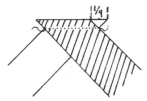

Figure 5-BS4.
Joining two bias strips with a ¼" seam.

Preparing and Applying Binding

Finishing the hem and neck edges with binding provides a neat finish on the curved edges, a visual finish to the edges, and extra body that enhances the fabric's drape.

1. Measure the length of edge to be bound, then cut and join bias strips to exceed that length by 8". For double-fold binding, cut the bias strips 2½" wide.
2. Press the binding in half lengthwise to make a continuous folded strip 1¼" wide.
3. At the starting end of the binding, open the strip and fold on the diagonal (Figure 5-B3). Trim to ¼" from the fold.

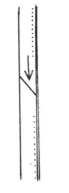

Figure 5-B3. Make a ¼" fold on the diagonal bias end.

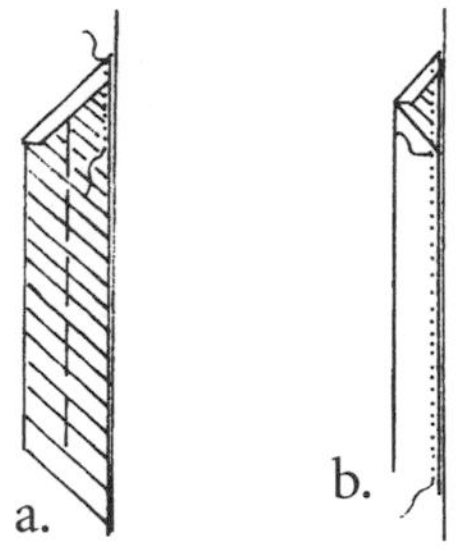

Figure 5-B4. a. Begin stitching on the lengthwise edge with bias unfolded for about 4". b. Refold the bias lengthwise (right sides out) and resume stitching through all thicknesses.

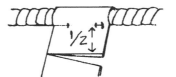

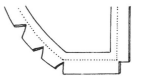

Figure 5-C1. Use a fabric strip wrapped around cord to determine the width needed for bias.

Figure 5-C5. Clip bias seam allowance to turn corners and curves.

4. Along a straight section on the right side of the chasuble top, place the raw edge of the binding flush to the raw edge of the chasuble. Using a ¼" seam and with the binding opened, sew the single layer of binding to the chasuble for about 4" (Figure 5-B4a). Lift the presser foot, return the binding to its folded position, and continue to stitch around the chasuble through all thicknesses (Figure 5-B4b).

5. With the needle in the fabric, stop about 2" before closing the circle and tuck the remaining end of the binding (trim if necessary) into the pocket formed by the binding at the starting point (Figure 5-B5). Continue to stitch through all thicknesses.

6. Wrap the binding over the raw edge to the inside of the chasuble, placing the folded edge of the binding on top of the stitching line. Blind stitch in place.

7. To close the circle when attaching open or unfolded binding (chapter 6) continue the stitching begun in step 4 without stopping to fold the binding over. When you come full circle, simply overlay the raw edge of the binding over the folded end and then sew the circle closed. The raw ends will be encased when the binding is folded over.

8. The same method may be used to finish a neck edge.

Figure 5-B5. Tuck the bias end into the pocket formed by the beginning end of the bias.

Constructing Cording

1. Determine the width of bias strips needed to cover the cable cord by wrapping a strip of fabric around the cord. Pin in place. Measure ½" out from the pin and trim the double thickness of the strip (Figure 5-C1). Unwrap the fabric strip from the cord and measure its trimmed size, which is the width to cut bias strips.

2. Measure the length of the fabric to be corded and add 12". Cut and join bias strips following the directions for bias strips.

3. Right side out, wrap the bias strip around the cording with the raw edges even and pin it in place. Using a zipper foot with the machine needle against the cording, stitch along the cording without crowding against it (Figure 5-C3).

4. Place the cording on the right side of the fabric. Align the cording stitching line along the seam line and the raw edges along the placement line or fabric raw edge. Baste using a zipper foot. To conceal the cording stitching, place the machine needle toward the cording, and stitch just inside the cording stitching by hugging close to the cording.

5. To round a curve, clip the raw edge of the cording, stopping at the stitching. To turn a corner, stop stitching just at the corner and clip to allow the cording to turn 90 degrees without cutting into the stitching (Figure 5-C5). Continue stitching using small stitches at the pivot.

Figure 5-C3. Use a zipper foot to stitch bias around cord.

6. To close a circle of cording, begin the cording in the same way described for binding steps 3 and 4. When you approach the close of the circle, trim the excess bias to ¼" longer than the bias fold at the beginning. Remove the cording stitching a few inches back and open out the bias strip. Cut the cable cord to meet the beginning end of the cord exactly—do not cut the bias. Unravel the cord ends and twist together (Figure 5-C6). Rewrap the cord with the bias strip and tuck the bias ends into the pocket formed at the beginning. Continue stitching to close the circle.

Figure 5-C6. To close a circle of cording, twist the threads together and then tuck bias into the pocket formed by the beginning end of the bias.

DRAFTING THE PATTERNS

The traditional set of vestments consists of five pieces: the chasuble, the stole, the maniple, the burse, and the chalice veil. With the order of deacon revived in the church, the set expands to include the deacon's stole. The "High Mass" set also includes the dalmatic and stole worn by the deacon and the tunicle worn by the subdeacon. Basic patterns and instructions for making the items are found in the following chapters:

Chapters 6 and 7: The traditional six-piece set of vestments, including a cowled medium chasuble, a fitted stole, a maniple, a Western-style deacon's stole, burse, and chalice veil.

Chapter 8: A traditional Y cross chasuble with tapered sleeves and an Eastern-style deacon's stole.

Chapter 9: The "High Mass" set, including a monastic style chasuble, dalmatic and tunicle, stoles, maniple, burse, and chalice veil.

Chapter 10: A stiffened chasuble, an overlay stole, and a child's chasuble.

Chapter 11: A painted overlay stole, a pieced, cotton chasuble for the warm summer months, and a pocket stole used for visitations.

The scale for the patterns is: one ³⁄₁₆" square equals 2", or 1" equal 10". All of the measurements given on the patterns are in inches. The patterns may be enlarged in a variety of ways as outlined below.

Remember to label each piece with all the necessary markings before cutting out the patterns. The seam allowances are included unless otherwise noted.

Methods for Enlarging the Patterns

1. Graph Paper

Enlarge the patterns by drawing them onto 1" gridded, pattern-tracing fabric or paper. Remember that one square of the pattern equals four (2" x 2") squares on the 1" grid. It may be helpful to draw in the lines of a 2" grid onto the fabric or paper before attempting to draft the pattern. Calculate how the lines fall within each occupied square of the pattern. Square by square, duplicate the lines in the corresponding square of the 2" grid. Pay special attention to the corners and curves, as well as to the intersection of pattern and grid lines.

2. Modified Coordinate

The patterns are essentially based on the rectangle. For example, the chasuble involves rounding the corners of a rectangle. A simple way to enlarge the patterns is to draw the specified size rectangle onto your pattern paper or fabric. Then place dots at the specified points where the x-coordinate (the measurement on the rectangle line) intersects with the y-coordinate (the measurement in from the rectangle line). Connect the dots to make the pattern line.

3. Projection

If you have access to an overhead projector, have a photocopier turn your pattern into a transparency. Tape a piece of paper to the wall that is large enough to accommodate the pattern. Position the projector the correct distance from the wall to make each square on the projected pattern grid measure 2". Draw the projected pattern onto the secured paper; the enlarged pattern will be perfectly scaled.

VESTMENT CONSTRUCTION BASICS

The Basic Chasuble

To make a plain, basic chasuble: Follow the pattern and directions for the child's chasuble found in chapter 10, only cut the chasuble larger to measure 44" to 60" wide by 90" to 120" total length (45" to 60" long in front and back). See Figure 6-1 on page 60 for directions on how to enlarge the neckline or use any of the neckline patterns in this book. For a simple tapered chasuble, use pattern 8 and omit the adorned orphreys.

Making the Stole

Guidelines

Use the pattern to cut two pieces each from the main fabric, lining and interfacing. To reduce bulk at seams, trim off the ½" seam allowance from the interfacing only.

The stole may be made from one continuous piece if the length is available. Normally, however, stoles have a center back seam. The stole may be a consistent width or it can be shaped at the neck by gradually curving 1" narrower for each 7" inches on either side of center back, which ensures a flat fit.

The ends of the stole may be slightly wider than the rest of the stole or of one continuous width. Crosses to match the center back "kissing cross" are a traditional adornment.

Simple crosses may be made from 4½" sections of braid. Apply the lengthwise pieces first, turning under the ends; then add the horizontal bars.

Apply ornamentation to the stole before adding linings. The stole may need to be mounted into a frame while the needlework is done.

To add fringe along the completed bottom edges, blind-stitch the fringe in place and turn it under at the outside edges.

Completing the Stole

1. Complete all ornamentation, then stitch the center back seams of the stole and the lining, when applicable. Attach a "kissing cross" at the center seam, if desired.
2. Lay the stole face down on a clean surface to attach the interfacing on the wrong side, following the instructions for interfacing above (page 48).
   By hand:
3. Press the stole to smooth the fabrics, then turn the ½" seam allowance in over the interfacing. Press and tack in place, and then mitre the corners.
4. Press the ½" seam allowance of the lining to the wrong side of the lining fabric. Pin the lining to the stole, wrong sides together, and stitch it in place using a blind slipstitch.
   By machine:
5. Press the fabrics, then lay the stole right side up on a smooth surface. Lay the lining over the stole, right sides together. Pin and stitch a ½" seam

along the stole perimeter, leaving a 6" opening along one straight inner edge.
6. Trim the corners, clip the neck curve, grade the seam, and turn the stole right side out by bringing the ends out through the opening. Press. Blind stitch the opening closed.

Creating the Maniple

Complete in the same manner as the stole except:
1. Cut one maniple piece on the fold from doubled fabric, lining, and interfacing.
2. Attach an elastic loop to the lining before attaching the lining to the maniple (it may be added after the maniple is complete, but it is easier to add it early on). Cut a piece of ¼" elastic that equals the measurement of the forearm plus 1", or 12". Overlap the ends of the elastic ½" and tack into a circle. Whip stitch the elastic to the center point of the right side of the maniple lining, with the tacked ends toward the maniple (Figure 5-M2). Over time the elastic tends to lose its stretch and may need to be replaced.
3. After completing the maniple, fold the maniple in half and measure down 7" from the center fold on both sides. Just at these 7" points, whip stitch the front and back together at the sides to hold the maniple in place when it's worn (Figure 5-M3).

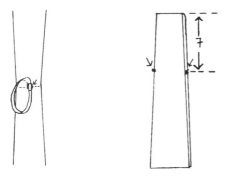

Figure 5-M2. Tack the elastic loop to the center of the lining.

Figure 5-M3. Securely tack the sides of the maniple together at the points shown (the 7" opening above the tacks are for the hand to slip through).

The Western Deacon's Stole

Guidelines

To size the stole for a comfortable and smooth fit across the chest and back, adjust the length of the sash

*Figure 5-D.
An alternative
deacon's stole.*

*Figure 5-D2.
Match the dots to seam
the stole sections.*

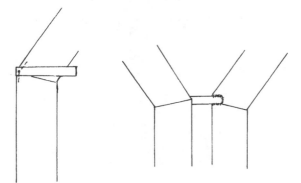

*Figure 5-D4.
Baste ribbon to the
right side of stole at seam.*

*Figure 5-D6.
Tack the remaining ribbon
end to the lining of the
opposing hip curve.*

(pattern section 1) to the measurement of the wearer from the left shoulder to the right hip (the pattern measures a 24" sash). A simple way to adjust the fit is to increase or decrease the ribbon that connects the front and back of the stole at the hip (see Figure 5-D4).

An alternative deacon's stole is the crossover stole, which fashions a straight (priest/bishop) stole worn off the left shoulder, is crossed over near the right knee, and is fastened with a decorative pin (Figure 5-D).

Cut two of both sections of the stole pattern from fabric, lining, and interfacing, unless instructed otherwise.

To complete the deacon's stole by hand, use the same method outlined for the priest's stole, but also insert a strip of ribbon between the layers at the hip seam.

The stole guidelines apply to the deacon's stole as well.

Completing the Western Deacon's Stole

1. Complete all ornamentation and attach the interfacing to the wrong side of the stole sections following the instructions above.
2. Stitch both sections 1 to sections 2 by placing the stole section ends right sides together and matching the dots (Figure 5-D2). Baste and check the seam to be sure the ornamentation lines up properly before stitching in a ½" seam. Press seam open.
3. Stitch the shoulder seams of the stole and the lining. Press seams open. Attach a "kissing cross" at shoulder seam, if desired.
4. Center a 6" piece of ribbon over the seam at the dot on the stole front, with right sides together and raw ends even (Figure 5-D4). Baste.
5. Continue in the same manner as for the stole, steps 5 and 6. Notch the outside corners at the section seam before turning.

6. Attach the remaining end of the ribbon to the seam on the lining side of the stole. Adjust the length (3" finished is average), fold under the end trimmed to ¼", and whip stitch in place (Figure 5-D6).

The Burse

Guidelines

The finished size ranges from an 8" to 12" square, depending on the size of the chalice and sanctuary.

Traditionally, the burse is lined in white linen.

Cut the burse boards (thin Plexiglas™ or bristol board) to within ⅛" less than finished size.

A basting glue stick is helpful for holding the seams while working.

Cut two squares each of fabric and lining, the finished size plus 1" for seams. (Cut 10" squares for a 9" burse.) If figured fabric is used, cut the squares to accommodate the fabric's design.

An alternate way to hinge the back side is to use 1" pieces of cording or ribbon placed every 2" beginning ½" in from the outside edge to equal five 1" hinges. Insert raw edges of cording or tape between the lining and fabric before stitching the back edges closed.

Completing the Burse

1. Adorn the top (usually at the center) and cord the outside edges, if desired.
2. Prepare the boards. If it's Plexiglas™, lightly smooth the edges with extra fine sandpaper or an emery board. If it's bristol board, use two layers for each square. Grade the boards by cutting two of the bristol boards ½" smaller overall to lessen the bulk along the outside edges. Glue one smaller

and one finished size square together, for both sets. Cover the outside surfaces with laminate or clear contact paper to protect the boards from moisture. Place the reduced bristol board on the lining side of the burse.

By hand:

3. Press in the fabric and lining squares ½" on all four sides to achieve finished size; mitre the corners.

4. Cover each board with a lining piece, wrapping the turned edges over the edges of the boards. Be sure fabric is stretched smooth but not so tight that the material is warped. Use the basting stick to secure along the raw edge, if needed.

5. Place the prepared fabric on the uncovered side of the boards, keeping the ends turned in. The fabric should cover the raw edges of the lining completely. Slip stitch the fabric to the lining on all four edges of both squares.

6. If the burse is not corded, a round braid may be added around the outer edges if desired.

7. Lay the two finished squares together, right sides out. If a figured fabric is used, take care that the top and bottom fabrics fall in the same direction. Whip stitch the two squares together along the back edge. Keep stitches loose enough for a flat fit when closed.

By machine:

8. Lay one fabric and one lining square right sides together and pin on three sides. Repeat with the remaining squares. Along the three pinned edges, stitch the lining to the fabric of each set in a ½" seam.

9. Trim the corners, grade the seam, and turn right sides out through the open end. Press flat and turn the open ends in ½".

10. Carefully slide the burse boards into the squares through the open side until you have a smooth, easy fit. Blind stitch the open ends closed.

12. Finish following "by hand" steps 6 and 7.

The Chalice Veil

Guidelines

The average finished size ranges from 22" to 24" square, depending on the size of the chalice. The patterns in this book are for a 24" square veil.

To determine the size of veil needed, add the size of the pall plus twice the height of the chalice (Figure 5-V).

Traditionally, chalice veils are lined in white linen.

Cut one fabric and one lining square. Do not interface.

Figure 5-V. Determine the size of the chalice veil by measuring the chalice height and the pall width.

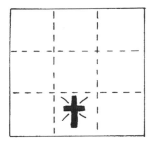

Figure 5-V1. The traditional placement of ornamentation.

Completing the Veil

1. Complete the desired ornamentation, traditionally placed at the center bottom (Figure 5-V1), and cord the outside edge, if desired.

By hand:

2. Press the fabric and lining squares in ½" on all four sides; mitre the corners.

3. Smooth the prepared fabric face down, keeping edges turned in. Smooth the lining right side up over the fabric so that the lining and fabric folded edges meet exactly. Baste. Slip stitch the fabric to the lining on all four edges.

4. If not corded, apply braid around the outer edges, if desired.

By machine:

5. Place the fabric and lining right sides together and pin the edges closed. Baste, leaving a 6" opening along one edge.

6. Stitch in a ½" seam along basted edges, leaving the opening.

7. Trim corners, grade the seam, and turn right sides out by pulling the veil through the 6" opening. Press smooth and iron the open edges in ½", even with the finished edge.

8. Blind stitch opening closed and apply braid around outer edges, if desired.

The Paraments: Altar Frontal, Bible Markers, and Pulpit Scarf

Guidelines

The measurements for these ornaments are determined by the width and height of the altar and the pulpit as well as the placement of carvings

The Bible markers are usually 24" long by 3" wide.

The Bible markers and the pulpit scarf may be made

in the same manner as the stole, but with one end left plain and open. To hold them in place on the lectern or pulpit, Velcro™ or weights are inserted at the plain ends before closing.

The paraments are usually made to match the vestments, or at least the liturgical season.

Use a good-bodied interfacing to assure a smooth, stable hang for each piece.

Basic Instructions for Making an Altar Frontal

1. Measure the altar to determine finished length and drop.
2. Cut fabric to size plus 1" in each direction for ½" seams. Cut the interfacing to exact size.
3. Cut lining the size of the frontal fabric plus the depth of the altar top plus an extra 3" for the hem (Figure 5-P3).
4. Adorn the frontal fabric and attach the interfacing to the wrong side.
5. Press under ½" along the top lengthwise edge of the frontal.
6. Smooth the lining out on a large surface, right side up. Smooth the frontal, right side down, over the lining, matching bottom and side edges. Baste. Stitch. Trim corners, turn it right side out, and press it smooth.
7. Slip stitch the top folded edge of the frontal to the lining extension.

8. Stitch a narrow hem on the remaining side edges of the lining.
9. Make a "sleeve" along the remaining lengthwise lining edge for the holding bar to pass through. To make the sleeve, after finishing the side edges of the lining, press the long unfinished edge under ½" and then fold over 2½" along the hemline (the altar depth). Blind stitch in place along the folded edge, leaving the side edges open for the bar to pass through. Check the size of your altar's bar: you may need to adjust the opening size to greater or lesser than 2½"—make this adjustment by altering the 3" added to the lining depth in step 3.

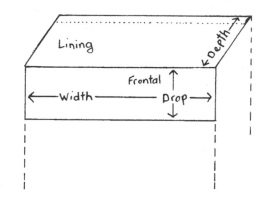

Figure 5-P3. The dimensions for determining the size of the frontal and its lining.

VESTMENT PLANNING SHEET

Vestments for: _____ Date: _____

Estimated completion date: _____

Vestments requested, size, and yardage:

___ Chasuble: length, front _____ back _____ width _____ yardage _____

____ lined? _____ matching binding? _____ yardage _____

___ Stole: type _____ length _____ width _____ yardage _____

___ Deacon's Stole: type _____ length _____ width _____ yardage _____

___ Maniple: length _____ width _____ forearm _____ yardage _____

___ Dalmatic: length _____ sleeve length _____ yardage _____

___ Tunicle: length _____ sleeve length _____ yardage _____

___ Burse: size: _____ yardage _____

___ Chalice Veil: size _____ yardage _____

___ Altar Frontal: altar length _____ drop _____ depth _____ yardage _____

___ Pulpit Scarf: width _____ drop _____ depth _____ yardage _____

___ Bible Markers (2): width _____ drop _____ depth _____ yardage _____

Total yardage: _____

Lining, if different _____

Setting: ___ Formal ___ Informal

Liturgical season: _____ Adornment: _____ non-specific _____ specific

Colors: Primary _____ Accent _____

Symbols: _____

Notes/notions: _____

PART II
THE PATTERNS

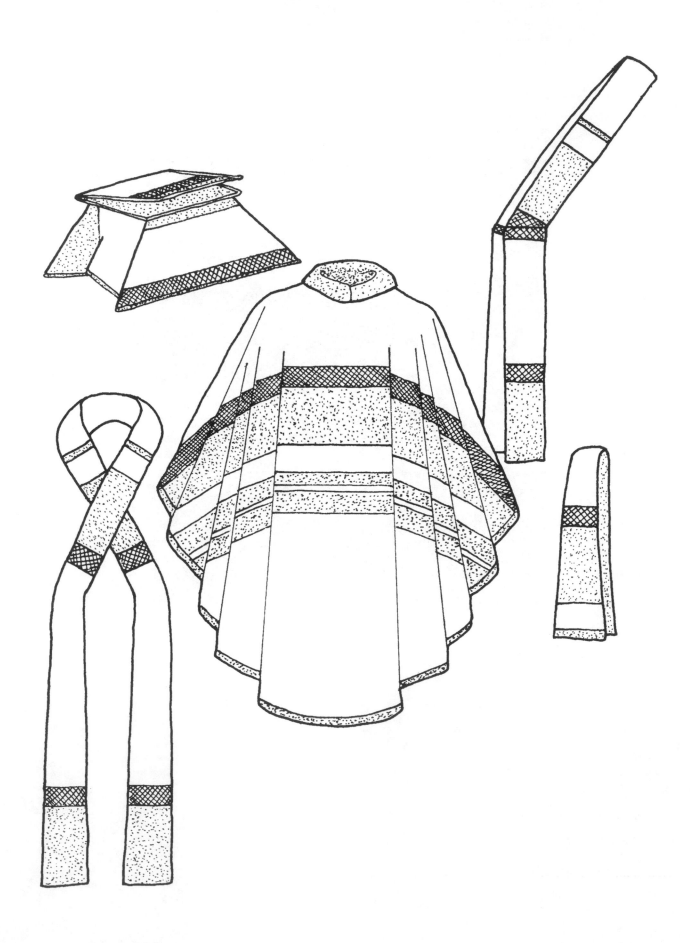

6.
ADVENT: BEGINNINGS IN RAW SILK

‿

When they make these sacred vestments for your brother Aaron and his sons to serve me as priests, they shall use gold, blue, purple, and crimson yarns, and fine linen.

—Exodus 28:4–5

The human family has created many ways of marking time, from observing the stars, the seasons of the year, and the phases of the moon, to creating calendars and clocks. The Christian church, too, marks time by using a calendar rooted in the life of Jesus, particularly his birth and resurrection. The Christian calendar sanctifies time and offers opportunities for introspection and growth.

The church year opens with the season of Advent, which focuses Christians on the presence of Christ. His coming is foretold in the Hebrew Scriptures and is chronicled in the Gospels of Matthew and Luke. The church also celebrates his coming in glory at the end of time, and his daily presence through prayer, the Word, sacrament, and neighbors. Advent is a time of expectation, vigilance, hope, and joy. Blue is the color associated with Advent because it represents the Virgin Mary, hope, and joyful expectation.

The main vestment described in this chapter is a medium or Gothic chasuble with a cowled collar and a horizontal design. It is made of raw silk, which is a good-bodied material with equal coloration on both sides, making it ideal for an unlined chasuble. It has self-enclosed seams to allow for piecing without lining. The other vestments discussed in the chapter are lined. The stole and maniple are of the tapered style, with the stole shaped to the neck. The deacon's stole is the fitted Western style. Using a rotary cutter, a ruler, and the mat-cutting method will ensure the best results for this project.

FABRIC REQUIREMENTS

Chasuble (60" wide by 52" long in front and back, finished)

Blue: 2½ yards of 60" wide material (does not allow for other pieces), or 5 yards of 44" wide material (includes enough yardage for the other pieces except the chalice veil).
Purple: 1¼ yards of 60" (allows for the stole), or 1⅔ yards of 44" (allows for the stole).
Red: ½ yard of 60" (enough for all other pieces except the deacon's stole), or ⅝ yard of 44" (allows for stole and maniple).
Interfacing: lightweight, ⅞ yard.

Stole (5" wide by 108" long, finished)

Blue: ⅔ yard of 60" wide material, or 1½ yards of 44" wide material.
Purple: ⅓ yard of either width.
Red: ⅛ yard of either width.
Interfacing: lightweight, 1¼ yards.
Purple embroidery floss to work the "kissing cross."

Maniple (4½" wide by 39" long, finished)

Blue: ¼ yard of either width.
Purple: ⅓ yard of 60" or ½ yard of 45".
Red: ⅛ yard of either width.

Interfacing: lightweight, 1¼ yards.
Elastic: ¼ yard of ¼".

Deacon's Stole (4½" wide, 24" sash and 27" tails, finished)

Blue: ⅔ yard of 60" wide material or 1½ yards of 44" wide material.
Purple: ⅓ yard of either width.
Red: ⅛ yard of either width.
Interfacing: lightweight, 1½ yards.
Ribbon: 6" of ¼" to 1" wide.

Burse (9" square, finished)

Blue: ¼ yard of either width.
Purple: ⅓ yard of either width.
Red: ⅛ yard of either width.
Plexiglas™: two 8½" squares.
Cording: 2½ yards of ¼" cording.

Chalice Veil (24" square, finished)

Blue: ¼ yard of 60" wide material or ⅜ yard of 44" wide material.
Purple: ¾ yard of either width (allows for the burse).
Red: ⅛ yard of either width.
Cording: 2¾ yards of ¼" cording.

AN UNLINED, COWLED CHASUBLE

Sizing

These directions are for a chasuble with a finished measurement of 60" wide by 52" long in front and back, suitable for a person about six feet tall.

To decrease the width, delete the amount needed for your correct size from the 60" cutting width. If you are making a chasuble 54" wide, cut all widths to 54".

Make length adjustments by reducing or lengthening the blue pieces, A and C. To size piece A: On the person who will wear the chasuble, estimate a pleasing position for the red stripe so that it falls equidistant from the top of the shoulder in front and back. Then measure the distance over the shoulder between the two red stripe positions. Add to this measurement 1½" for the ¾" seam allowances. The total is the size to cut piece A.

The two C pieces may be shortened or lengthened by the remaining amount needed for adjustment. If you reduced piece A by 2" and you want an overall measurement of 48", reduce each C piece by 2" (52"

less 2" makes 50"; therefore, 2" inches more are needed to reduce to 48"). C pieces need not be exact since they can be adjusted when you cut out the chasuble pattern, but do be aware that if you need more length, you must add it to the C pieces when you prepare your yardage (see Figure 6-C14).

To reduce or enlarge the neck opening, add to or decrease the cut edge by the same amount around the diameter of the neck opening and along the inside edge of the cowl collar (Figure 6-1).

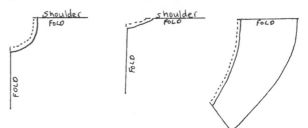

Figure 6-1. To alter neck opening, add or reduce by an equal amount on chasuble front and back neck lines and on the collar.

Prepare the Yardage

For this chasuble you will cut fabric from several colors, piece them together in the order given, and then lay the chasuble pattern over the pieced length in order to cut out the chasuble.

If you are using a fabric less than 60" wide, you will need to piece each section listed below to obtain the required 60" width. For example, if you are using a 36" silk, you will need to cut two 20½" by 36" pieces and then stitch them together in order to cut piece A; or, if you are using a 44" fabric, you will need to cut 1½ widths at 20½" long, and then stitch them together in order to cut piece A.

1. Cut the following:

Fabric	Section	Quantity	Size
Blue	A	one	20½" x 60"
Blue	B	two	4¾" x 60"
Blue	C	two	30" x 60"
Purple	D	two	11" x 60"
Purple	E	two	1¾" x 60"
Purple	F	two	3" x 60"
Purple	I	one	29" x 12"
Red	G	two	3" x 60"
Red	J	one	29" x 12"

2. On the two purple D sections, measure and draw a line 2¼" in from one 60" raw edge. Right sides together, align one raw edge of the red strips G along the drawn lines (Figure 6-C2). Pin in

Figure 6-C2. Placement of red strip G along the drawn line on the purple D.

place. Stitch ½" from the aligned edges of the red strips G.

3. Press the seams to relax the stitching, then press the red strips G toward the purple D raw edge to conceal the seams. The remaining raw edges of the red strips will be ¼" short of the purple D raw edges. Baste in place (Figure 6-C3).

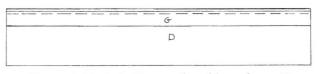

Figure 6-C3. Strip G pressed and basted over D with ¼" of D extending past G.

4. With right sides together, align the basted raw edge of the red strip G to a 60" raw edge of the blue piece A (the ¼" purple D extension will extend beyond the aligned edges). Pin in place. Stitch ½" from the aligned raw edges. Press to relax the closed seam.

5. Press the ¼" purple D extension over the raw edges of the completed seam to enclose the raw edges (Figure 6-C5). Stitch the purple flap in place. Repeat steps 4 and 5 with the remaining stitched and basted red strip G and blue A 60" raw edge. Press the enclosed seams toward piece A. You now have a joined section of D-G-A-G-D measuring 40" by 60". Set it aside.

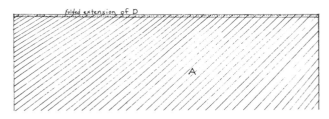

Figure 6-C5. The ¼" extension of D folded and stitched to enclose raw edges of seam.

6. On the two blue B sections, measure and draw a line 1½" in from one 60" raw edge. Right sides together, align one raw edge of the purple E strips along the drawn lines (in the same manner as Figure 6-C2). Pin it in place. Stitch ¼" from the aligned edges of the purple E strips.

7. Press the seams to relax the stitching, then press the purple E strips toward the blue B raw edges. The remaining raw edges of the purple E strips will be ¼" short of the blue B raw edges. Baste in place (in the same manner as Figure 6-C3).

8. Stitch B to D-G-A-G-D by using a French (self-enclosed) seam as follows: With wrong sides together, match the remaining 60" raw edge of a blue B section to a 60" raw edge of the D-G-A-G-D section completed in step 5. Pin. Stitch in a ¼" seam. Press to relax the seam, then fold the right sides together of B and D-G-A-G-D exactly along the seam line. Press and pin in place. Stitch ½" from the folded edge to encase the ¼" seam (Figure 6-C8). Press to relax the seam, then press the seam toward the blue section. Repeat using the remaining blue B section and D-G-A-G-D 60" raw edge. You now have a joined piece, E-B-D-G-A-G-D-B-E, with ¼" of B extending beyond E.

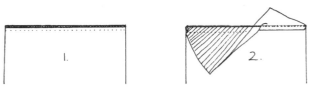

Figure 6-C8. The French seam.
1. Wrong sides together, stitch in a ¼" seam.
2. Fold fabrics right sides together; exactly along the seam line, stitch in a ½" seam to enclose raw edges.

9. Press under ½" on one 60" raw edge of the two purple F sections. Measure and draw a line 2½" in from a 60" raw edge of the two blue C sections. Right sides together, align the unturned raw edge of the purple F strips along the drawn lines (in the same manner as Figure 6-C2). Pin in place. Stitch ½" from the aligned edges of the purple F strips.

10. Press the seams to relax the stitching, then press the purple F strips toward the blue C raw edges—maintaining the pressed-under edges on sections F. Blue sections C will extend 1" beyond the folded edges of F (Figure 6-C10). Baste F in place. Blind stitch by hand along the folded edges.

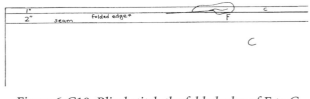

Figure 6-C10. Blind stitch the folded edge of F to C with 1" of C extending beyond F.

11. Join section C-F to E-B-D-G-A-G-D-B-E using a French seam. With wrong sides together, align the ¼" extending raw edge of a blue B section to the 1" extending raw edge of a blue C. Pin. Stitch in a ¼" seam. Press to relax the seam, then fold exactly along the seam so that the right side of C-F is facing the right side of E-B-D-G-A-G-D-B-E. Press and pin in place. Stitch ½" from the folded edge to encase the ¼" seam. Press to relax the seam, then press the seam toward section C-F. Repeat using the remaining C-F section and the remaining

E-B-D-G-A-G-D-B-E raw edge. You have now joined all of the pieces into one section H, consisting of C-F-C-E-B-D-G-A-G-D-B-E-C-F-C (see Figure 6-C14) and are ready to cut your pattern.

Cut the Pattern

12. Following the general instructions for pattern enlarging, page 50, draft the chasuble pattern 6 and the cowl neck pattern 6. If you made size adjustments to the chasuble pieces when you cut

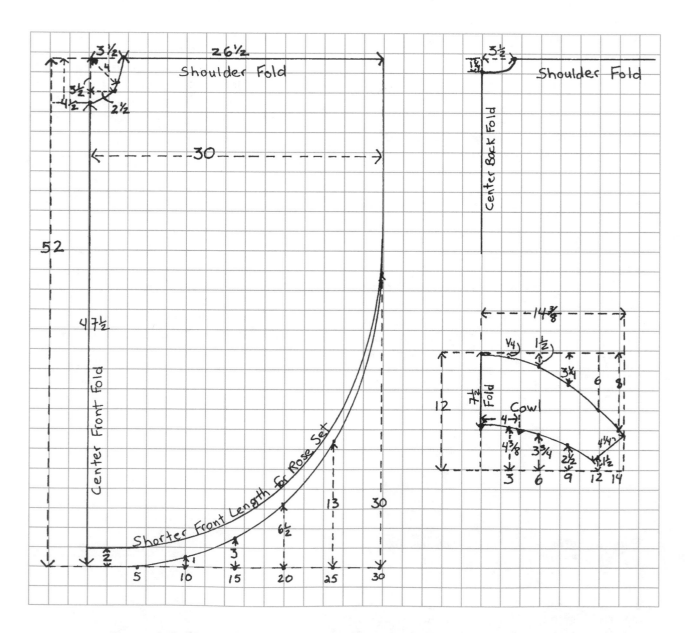

Pattern 6. Gothic (medium) chasuble with cowl collar and front and back neck lines.
Scale: one square = 2 inches. Cut one chasuble and one collar on folds.

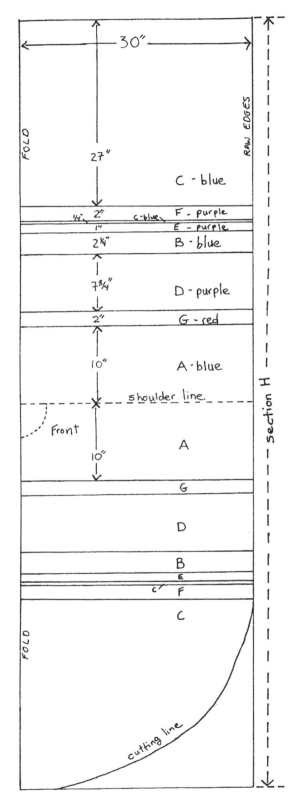

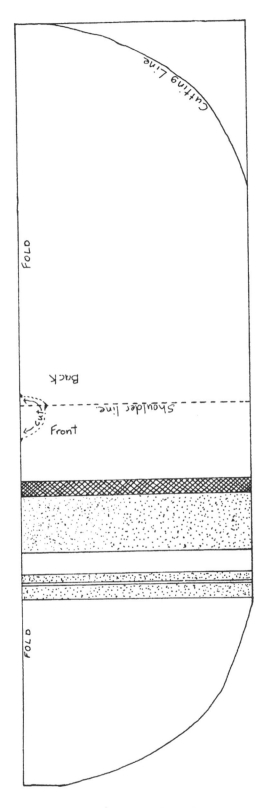

Figure 6-C14.
Pattern 6 aligned with the shoulder line and center fold.

Figure 6-C15. Pattern 6 flipped over and realigned with shoulder line and center fold.

them, be sure the pattern reflects the same changes.

13. Fold pieced H in half lengthwise, making sure all the seams are lined up exactly crosswise. With pins, lightly mark the shoulder line that divides blue A in half, 10" from each seam A-G (see Figure 6-C14). Trim any uneven edges that may have formed during the piecing.

14. Lay chasuble pattern 6 on H, aligning the top (shoulder edge) of the pattern along the shoulder line marked in step 13 and the folded edge along the center fold (Figure 6-C14). Cut along the bottom curved edge. Trace the front neck line that extends from the center fold and shoulder line.

15. Flip the pattern over, maintaining the pattern alignment at the shoulder line, but extending on the fold line along the remaining half of the center fold (Figure 6-C15). Cut along the bottom curved edge. Trace the back neck line extending from the center fold and shoulder line.

16. Mark the center front, center back, and shoulder lines with small notches. Cut out the neckline and notches along the traced lines. Remove the pins marking the shoulder line. Set the chasuble aside.

17. Fold the purple piece I in half crosswise to make a rectangle 14½" by 12". Lay the cowl collar pattern on the purple I, aligning the folded edge to the fold edge on the pattern (Figure 6-C17). Cut out along the outside cutting lines. Include notches at the shoulder lines and center back (the fold). Repeat using red piece J and lightweight interfacing.

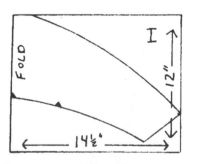

Figure 6-C17. Layout for cowl collar.

Finishing the Neckline

18. Attach the interfacing to the neck facing J following the general instructions on page 48.

19. Fold the neck piece I, right sides together, in half crosswise (in the same way you cut it out). Pin the short straight cut edges together. Stitch in a ⅝"

seam. Press the seam open. Repeat with the collar facing J.

20. Press under ⅝" along the inside curved edge of I, clipping where necessary for a smooth fold.

21. With right sides together, align the center seams and outside curved raw edges of I and J. Pin along the outside curve and stitch in a ½" seam. Grade the seam and clip curves. Press the seam to relax it. Fold the right side out along the seam line and press it flat.

22. Stay stitch the chasuble neck edge by stitching within a scant ⅝" from the cut edge.

23. With right sides together, pin the collar facing J to the chasuble neckline, matching the center front seam to the center front notch and the notched center backs and shoulder lines. Stitch in a ⅝" seam, keeping piece I free (Figure 6-C23). Trim and clip the seam, then press the seam toward the cowl.

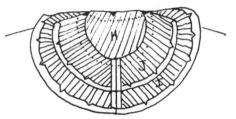

Figure 6-C23. Stitch cowl collar to neck opening, keeping facing I free.

24. Pin the outside folded edge of I to the inside of the chasuble neck seam, placing the fold at the stitching line. Blind stitch in place.

Finishing the Hemline

25. Cut and join two continuous bias strips of purple 2½" wide by 120" long (see general directions on page 48) and two red bias strips 2½" wide by 25" long. Join one of the purple bias strips to one of the red strips. Repeat with the remaining purple and red strips. Press the red strips under ¼" along their raw diagonal ends (see Figure 5-B3, page 49). Press the bias strips in half lengthwise, then press under ¼" along one continuous cut edge of both strips.

26. Unfold the length of the bias strips and, with right sides together, pin the unpressed edge of the bias strips to the outside chasuble edge. Begin by pinning the folded red bias ends at a D-G seam so that the red bias extends over section A to the opposing G-D seam (Figure 6-C26). Continue to pin the rest of the bias strips all the way around

Figure 6-C26. Bias-bound hem, with red strips extending across A to seams G-D.

the chasuble. To close the circle, lay the purple ends over the folded red bias ends and trim the excess purple, if necessary (see binding step 7 on page 49). Stitch the bias strips to the chasuble in a ¼" seam, keeping the folded edge free. Press the seam toward the binding.

27. Refold the bias edging in half along the crease so that the ¼" folded edge of the bias falls along the seam line. Pin. Blind stitch in place.

A Tapered Stole

Prepare the Yardage

You will cut and piece several colors of fabric together and then cut the pieced unit lengthwise to make two identical strips before cutting out the pattern.

1. Cut the following:

Fabric	Section	Quantity	Size
Blue	L	one	20" x 12"
Blue	M	one	3" x 12"
Blue	N	one	13" x 12"
Blue	O	two	56" x 6"
Purple	P	one	9½" x 12"
Purple	Q	one	8" x 12"
Purple	R	one	1" x 12"
Red	S	two	2½" x 12"

2. Using ¼" seams, piece the cut sections in the following order: N to R, M to Q, one S to L, the other S to P. Then join R to M and L to the other S that is connected to P. Now join Q to the remaining S with a 12" cut edge. You now have a single piece, N-R-M-Q-S-L-S-P (Figure 6-S2). Press all the seams toward purple P.

3. Cut the joined piece N-R-M-Q-S-L-S-P in half lengthwise to make two 6" by 56" strips.

Cut the Pattern

4. Draft the pattern (page 66) following the general instructions (see page 50).

5. With wrong sides together, lay the two strips N-R-M-Q-S-L-S-P so that the piecing matches exactly (flower head pins are helpful here). Overlay the stole pattern, making the bottom edge of the stole pattern flush with the

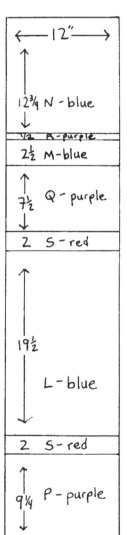

Figure 6-S2. The stole piecing.

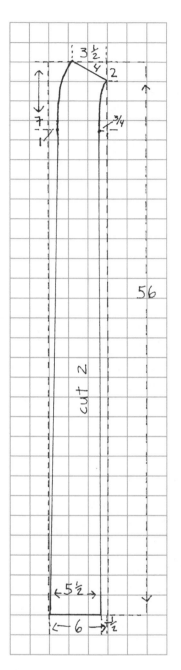

Pattern 6. Tapered stole with fitted neck line. Cut two.
Scale: one square = 2 inches.

bottom edges of P. Cut out following the stole pattern lines (Figure 6-S5).

Making the Stole

6. Remove the pattern and pin sections N together at the neck edge, right sides together, to make one continuous piece. Stitch using a ½" seam. Press the seam open.

7. On the right side of the neck seam, draw a cross by marking 1" in from the inner curve and 1½" in from the outer curve of the stole. Draw a 1" line perpendicular to the seam 1½" in from the inner curve so that the two arms extend ½" from seam. Using three strands of purple embroidery floss, work a "kissing cross" in cross-stitch (Figure 6-S7).

8. Using the stole pattern, cut O, the stole facing, from the blue pieces. Cut the interlining from a 56" by 12" piece of lightweight interfacing. Attach the interlining to the facing following the general instructions on page 48. Stitch the neck seam; press it open.

9. Complete the stole by hand or by machine, following general stole instructions, page 51.

A TAPERED MANIPLE

Prepare the Yardage

You will cut and piece several colors of fabric together before cutting out the pattern.

Figure 6-S5.
Pattern layout
over piecing.

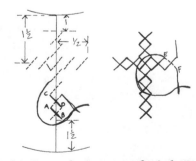

Figure 6-S7. Cross placement and stitch. Bring needle up at A and down at B, up at C then down at D; repeat across whole row. Work back by bringing needle up at E and down at F.

1. Cut the following:

Fabric	Section	Quantity	Size
Blue	T	one	3" x 12"
Blue	U	one	14" x 6"
Purple	V	one	1½" x 12"
Purple	W	one	8" x 12"
Purple	X	one	40" x 6"
Red	Y	one	2½" x 12"

2. Using ¼" seams, with right sides together, piece V to T, W to Y. Then join T to W. You now have a single piece, V-T-W-Y (Figure 6-M2). Press all the seams toward purple V.

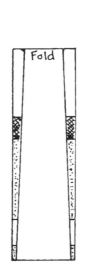

Figure 6-M2.
First set of the maniple piecing.

3. Cut the joined piece V-T-W-Y in half lengthwise to make two 6" by 13½" strips. Join one raw end of Y to blue piece U. Repeat using the other end of U and the remaining Y end. You now have a single piece, V-T-W-Y-U-Y-W-T-V, which measures 6" by 40" (Figure 6-M3). Press the seams in same direction as the other seams.

Cut the Pattern

4. Draft the pattern following the general instructions, page 50.
5. Fold V-T-W-Y-U-Y-W-T-V in half crosswise to measure 6" by 20", with the piecing matching exactly (use flower head pins to hold it in place). Overlay the maniple pattern with the top fold edge of the maniple pattern flush with the folded edge of U (Figure 6-M5). Cut out the maniple following the pattern lines.

Making the Maniple

6. Using the maniple pattern, cut the maniple facing from the purple piece X, folded in half crosswise.

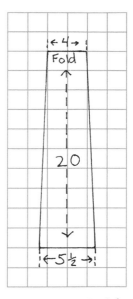

Figure 6-M5.
Maniple pattern
layout.

Pattern 6. Maniple.
Cut one on fold.
Scale: one square = 2 inches.

Cut the interlining from a folded 40" by 6" piece of lightweight interfacing. Attach interlining to facing following general instructions, page 48.

7. Complete the maniple by hand or by machine following the general maniple instructions, page 51.

A WESTERN DEACON'S STOLE

Sizing

The directions are for a completed deacon's stole measuring 24" from the left shoulder to where it catches under the right arm (the sash section). It fits a person around 5'9" tall and 150 pounds. You may need to shorten or lengthen the girth for a comfortable and smooth fit across the chest and back. A simple way to do so is to increase or decrease the ribbon that connects the front and back of the stole under the

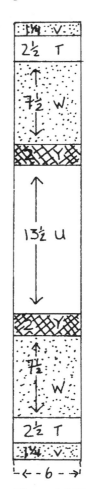

Figure 6-M3.
The maniple piecing.

arm (see Figure 5-D4, page 52). Or, if you prefer to adjust the actual length of the stole, reduce or lengthen the blue piece DC.

If the bottom section of the stole needs lengthening or shortening, adjust piece DA at the time of piecing and/or piece DF when you cut the stole from the pattern. Piece DF need not be exact since it can be adjusted at the time of cutting out the stole pattern, but if more length is needed, it must be added to DF when it is cut out.

Prepare the Yardage

Cut and piece several colors of fabric together to make one long strip for the sash and two identical shorter strips for the tails before cutting out the pattern.

1. Cut the following:

Fabric	Section	Quantity	Size
Blue	DA	one	16" x 11"
Blue	DB	one	3" x 11"
Blue	DC	one	24" x 5½"
Blue	DD	one	50" x 5½"
Blue	DE	two	28" x 5½"
Purple	DF	one	8" x 11"
Purple	DG	one	8" x 11"
Purple	DH	one	1" x 11"
Red	DI	one	2½" x 11"
Red	DJ	two	3" x 11"

2. Using ¼" seams and with right sides together, piece the cut sections in the following order: DF to DI, DA to one of the DJ pieces, the other DJ to DG, and DB to DH. Then join DI to DA and DG to DB. You now have two pieces: DF-DI-DA-DJ and DJ-DG-DB-DH (Figure 6-D2). Press all the seams toward purple DF and DG.

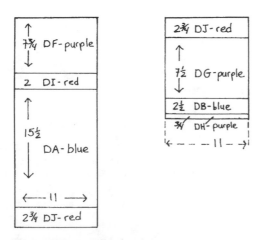

Figure 6-D2. Piecing for the deacon's stole in two units.

3. Cut the joined pieces DF-DI-DA-DJ in half lengthwise to make two 5½" by 28" strips and DJ-DG-DB-DH in half lengthwise to make two 5½" by 13½" strips.

4. With right sides together, join the remaining end of one DH section to one end of DC. On the other end of DC, join the remaining DH section to make one continuous strip measuring 5½" by 50" (Figure 6-D4). Press the seams toward DC and fold in half crosswise to measure 5½" by 2", matching piecing exactly (flower head pins are helpful here).

Cut the Pattern

5. Draft the deacon's stole pattern following the general instructions on page 50.

6. Overlay the sash, section 1 of the stole pattern, on the folded-over 50" piece (see Pattern 6), matching the fold line to the folded edge. The width should match exactly. Cut the bottom edge at its angle. Mark a dot for matching and for placing the ribbon on section 2. Using the same pattern piece, cut the lining from blue piece DD and mark a dot. Center the pattern over a strip of interfacing, 5" by 50", cut bottom angled edges, and trim ¼".

7. With wrong sides together, align strips DF-DI-DA-DJ so that the piecing matches exactly. Overlay pattern section 2 with the bottom edges flush. Cut the top angled edge. Mark a dot for matching to section 1. Using the same pattern piece, cut the lining from blue pieces DE and mark a dot. Center the pattern over a strip of 5" by 28" interfacing and cut the top angled edge. Trim ½" from bottom end of interfacing.

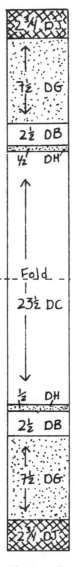

Figure 6-D4. Piecing for section 1 of the deacon's stole.

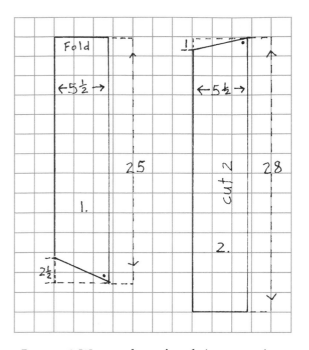

Pattern 6. Western deacon's stole in two sections. Cut one section 1 on fold and two from section 2. Scale: one square = 2 inches.

Making the Deacon's Stole

8. Attach interfacing sections to facing sections following general instructions, page 48.
9. Complete the stole by hand or by machine, following general stole instructions on page 51.

A Corded Burse

Prepare the Yardage

You will cut and piece several colors of fabric together to make the square top. Cording is used to finish the edges.

1. Cut the following:

Fabric	Section	Quantity	Size
Blue	BA	one	5½" x 19"
Purple	BB	one	2½" x 19"
Purple	BC	two	9½" x 9½"
Red	BD	one	2½" x 19"

2. Using ¼" seams and with right sides together, piece BA to BD, then BD to BB. You now have a single piece, BA-BD-BB (Figure 6-B2). Press all the seams toward purple BB.
3. Cut the joined piece BA-BD-BB in half crosswise to make two 9½" squares for the burse covers.
4. From the remaining blue fabric, cut and join bias

*Figure 6-B2.
Piecing for the burse.*

strips to make 2½ yards by 2". Make 2½ yards of ¼" cording following general instructions, page 49.

Making the Burse

5. Cut the cording into two 1¼-yard lengths and attach it to the outside edge of the burse covers. See general instructions (page 49) for attaching the cording and for closing the circle smoothly.
6. Finish the burse according to the general instructions, page 52. Use pieces BC for the lining and a whipstitch around the cording along one edge to attach the two covers (Figure 6-B6).

Figure 6-B6. Whip stitch around cording to join burse covers.

A Corded Chalice Veil

Prepare the Yardage

You will cut and piece several colors of fabric together to make the square top. Cording is added to finish the edges.

1. Cut the following:

Fabric	Section	Quantity	Size
Blue	CA	two	6½" x 24½"
Purple	CB	one	1½" x 24½"
Purple	CC	one	9¼" x 24½"
Purple	CD	one	24½" square
Red	CE	one	2¾" x 24½"

2. Using ¼" seams and with right sides together, piece one 24½" edge of a CA to CB and the other CA to CC. Then join the remaining 24½" edge of the CA that is joined with CC to the remaining long edge of CB. Now join CE to the remaining long edge of CA. You now have a single piece, CC-CA-CB-CA-CE, which measures 24½" square for the

chalice veil (Figure 6-V2). Press all the seams toward purple CC.

3. From the remaining purple fabric, cut and join bias strips to make a 100" by 2" strip. Make 100" of ¼" cording following the general instructions, page 49.

Making the Chalice Veil

4. Attach the cording to the outside edges of the chalice veil. See general instructions (page 50) for closing the circle of the cording smoothly.

5. Finish the chalice veil according to general instructions on page 53. Use piece CD for the lining.

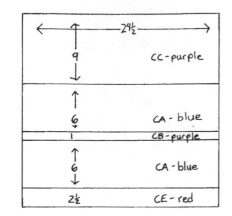

Figure 6-V2.
Piecing for the chalice veil.

NOTES

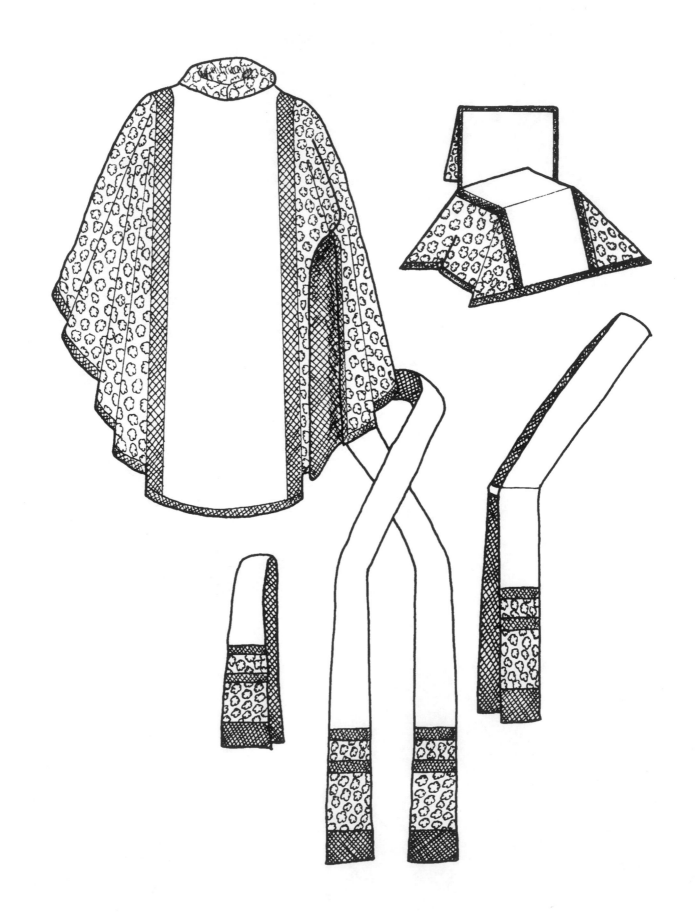

7.
THE ROSE SET:
3 ADVENT AND 4 LENT

༄

Glory in his holy name; let the hearts of those who seek the
LORD *rejoice.*

—Psalm 105:3

Advent and Lent are liturgical seasons that call us back to God to repent and to seek God's presence. They are demanding seasons because we are asked to live our lives more intentionally, day in and day out. One way we do this is by fasting. We deny ourselves the ways of the world to seek grace more diligently and to prepare ourselves to meet God. The Third Sunday of Advent and the Fourth Sunday of Lent are transitional Sundays that mark the midpoint of Advent and Lent. "Rejoice! You are halfway there. The light is visible at the end." To signal the transition from penitence to the coming light of Christ, rose-colored vestments may be worn on these two Sundays.

The rose set described below takes advantage of the narrow Japanese fabrics, such as the *obi* or *yukata*, which normally are 14½" inches wide. Finely woven with excellent body and color, these fabrics are ideal to use down the center length of a chasuble. The chasuble sleeve is made from a delicate, embossed silk. Normally such a silk is not recommended, but by quilting it to the silk lining, it may be used effectively. Rather than a separate border, the lining is folded over the chasuble top to complete the outer edge. The patterns are the same as those used for the blue Advent set, except that the back is longer than the front and it features a vertical design. The lining contrasts with the chasuble materials.

Since it will be used as the chasuble foundation, be sure to purchase a stable, good-bodied silk lining For highly delicate silks, you may need to sandwich a lightweight interlining between the chasuble top and the lining (see interlining guidelines on page 46). Do this by overlaying the interlining on the wrong side of the lining, basting it in place, and proceeding as if the interlining and lining are one fabric.

FABRIC REQUIREMENTS

Chasuble (58" wide by 51" long in front and 53" long in back, finished)

Fabric A: 3 yards of Japanese or other narrow width (14½") fabric.

Fabric B: 3⅓ yards of at least 42" wide compatible silk fabric for sleeves and cowled collar.

Fabric C: 6 yards of 60" wide contrasting silk for the orphreys, collar, and chasuble lining (allows for all of the vestment pieces) or 6 yards of 44" fabric pieced to make a 60" width for the lining (allows for all items except the chalice veil and deacon's stole lining) or 3 yards of 60" lining fabric and 6 yards of 2½" wide ribbon or braid for the orphreys.

Interfacing: lightweight, ⅞ yard.

Stole (5" wide by 108" long, finished)

Fabric A: 1¼ yards of Japanese or other narrow-width fabric.

Fabric B: ¼ yard of a compatible silk.

Fabric C: 1⅝ yards of contrasting silk for ornaments and lining.

Interfacing: lightweight, 1¼ yards.

Embroidery floss: in a contrasting color to work a "kissing cross," if desired.

Maniple (4½" wide by 39" long, finished)

Fabric A: ½ yard of Japanese or other narrow fabric (allows for the burse).
Fabric B: ⅛ yard of a compatible silk.
Fabric C: ⅛ yard of 60" contrasting silk for the ornaments and lining or ¼ yard of 44" wide silk.
Interfacing: lightweight, 1¼ yards.
Elastic: ¼ yard of ¼".

Deacon's Stole (4½" wide, 24" sash, and 27" tails, finished)

Fabric A: 1½ yards of Japanese or other narrow width fabric.
Fabric B: ¼ yard of a compatible silk.
Fabric C: ⅓ yard of 60" contrast silk for the ornaments and lining or 1½ yards of 44" wide silk
Interfacing: lightweight, 1½ yards.
Ribbon: 6" of ¼" to 1" wide.

Burse (9" square, finished)

Fabric A: ¼ yard of Japanese or other narrow-width fabric.
Fabric B: ⅓ yard of a compatible silk for lining.
Fabric C: ⅛ yard of contrast silk for ornaments.
Plexiglas™: two thin 9" squares.

Chalice Veil (24" square, finished)

Fabric A: ⅔ yard of Japanese or other narrow-width fabric.
Fabric B: ⅔ yard of a compatible silk.
Fabric C: ⅔ yard of contrast silk for ornaments and lining.

A LINED, COWLED CHASUBLE

Sizing

Make size adjustments when drafting and cutting the pattern. The width may be adjusted by altering the width of the center panel or by reducing the sleeve width.

Prepare the Yardage

The chasuble is constructed by using a "sew and flip" method; that is, the chasuble top is pieced as it is stitched to the lining foundation.
  1. Cut the following pieces:
    From fabric A: Cut the length to 104", or the exact total desired for the finished length from hem to hem. These instructions assume a 14" width (a 14½" *yukata* with the selvages removed).
    From fabric B: Cut two 106" by 20" pieces. An adjustment to this width may be necessary if your central panel or desired finished width is different from these instructions. You may determine the width needed by taking half of the width of your central panel plus 2½" (the finished orphrey width) and subtracting this total from half the desired width of the chasuble.
    From fabric C: Cut two 3" by 104" (or your exact total finished length) strips and a 3-yard length of the 60" lining width.

    Cut the pattern:

2. Following the general instructions for pattern enlarging on page 50, draft the chasuble and the cowls patterns from chapter 6 (page 62). Add one extra inch to the entire perimeter of the chasuble pattern for the hem overlay.
3. Fold the 60" lining width in half lengthwise, matching selvage edges. Lightly mark with pins the shoulder line, which falls at 54" or at the midpoint from the cut 3-yard length (see Figure 7-C4).
4. Lay the chasuble pattern 6 on the lining fabric, aligning the top (shoulder edge) of the pattern along the shoulder line marked in step 3 and the folded edge along the center fold (Figure 7-C4). Cut along the bottom curved edge. On the right side of the fabric, trace the back neck line extending from the center fold to the shoulder line.
5. Flip the pattern over, maintaining pattern alignment at the shoulder line but extending the fold line along the remaining half of the center fold (Figure 7-C5). Cut the 2" shorter front length along the bottom curved edge. On the right side of the fabric, trace the front neck line extending from the center fold to the shoulder line.
6. Transfer the neck lines to the flip right side so that the whole neck line is drawn onto the right side of the fabric. On the wrong side, draw the shoulder lines.
7. Lay the two cut sleeve lengths B wrong sides together and temporarily mark your shoulder lines on both sections at the midpoint, or 53" from the cut 106" length. Omit from the pattern the 1" perimeter hem allowance added for the lining. Lay the modified pattern on the sleeve fabric aligning the top (shoulder edge) of the pattern along the marked shoulder line and the widest

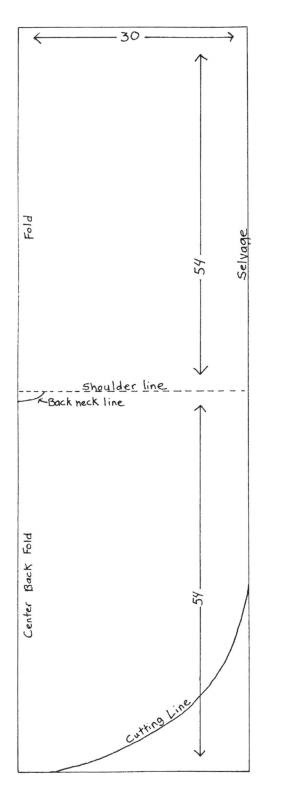

Figure 7-C4.
Pattern layout for chasuble back.

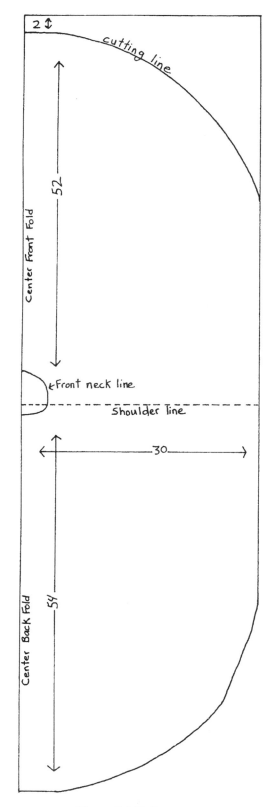

Figure 7-C5. Pattern
layout for chasuble front.

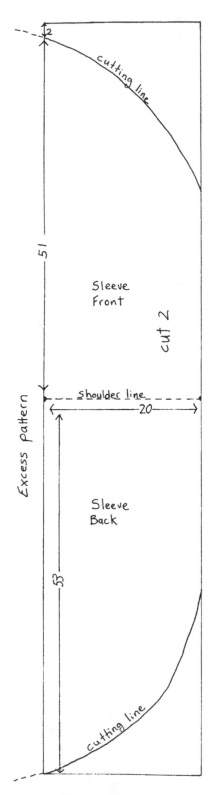

Figure 7-C8. Pattern layout for chasuble sleeves.

point of the sleeve width along one cut edge (see Figure 7-C8). Cut along the bottom curved edge.

8. Flip over the pattern, maintaining the pattern alignment at the shoulder line, but extending the pattern along the remaining half of the cut length. Cut the shorter length along the bottom curved edge (Figure 7-C8). Notch shoulder lines. Put a small "F" within ½" of the outside cut edge to help you identify the front from the back.

9. Fold the remaining length (about ⅓ yard) of fabric B in half crosswise. Lay the cowl collar pattern on the fabric by aligning the fold line on the pattern to the folded edge (Figure 7-C9). Cut along the cutting lines. Cut notches to mark the shoulder lines and center back. Repeat using the lining fabric and light-weight interfacing.

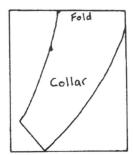

Figure 7-C9. Pattern layout for cowl collar.

Making the Chasuble

10. Smooth the chasuble lining on a large, clean flat surface with the wrong side up. With wrong sides together, center fabric A over the lining. Fabric A should fall 1" short of the chasuble at both ends and be equidistant from the sleeve edges (see Figure 7-C11). Pin, then baste in place. Trim fabric A to within 1" of the lining bottom curved edge, if needed.

11. Sew and flip the orphreys. Right sides together, lay the orphrey strips along the edges of the central panel (Figure 7-C11). Pin and baste in place. Using thread to match the lining, stitch the orphreys to A in a ¼" seam, stitching through all thicknesses. Press to relax the seams, then press the orphreys outward and baste. Trim the orphreys to within 1" of the curved edge at the bottom.

12. Sew and flip the sleeves. Align the inside straight edge of a sleeve B piece to the remaining cut edge of an orphrey, matching shoulder lines and the front to within 1" of the lining edge and the back to within 1" of the back edge (Figure 7-C12). Pin and baste in place. Stitch the sleeve to the orphrey in a ¼" seam through all thicknesses. Press to relax seam and press sleeve outward. Repeat with the remaining sleeve B and orphrey.

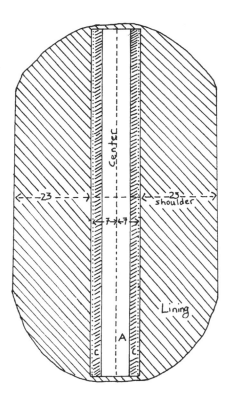

Figure 7-C11. The placement of center panel A and orphrey strips C on the lining for stitching.

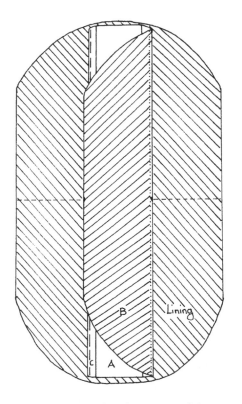

Figure 7-C12. The placement of sleeve B on an orphrey C and the lining for stitching.

13. Smooth the chasuble over the lining on a large, clean flat surface. The chasuble lining should extend 1" beyond the chasuble top around the whole perimeter. If not, trim accordingly. Pin and baste the sleeve in place. By hand, quilt the sleeve to the lining using thread to match the sleeve. See Figure 7-C13 for the quilting lines. If your fabric is stable enough to quilt by machine, use a walking foot and quilt outward by working from the center of the chasuble toward the sleeve edges.

Finishing the Hemline

14. Press the 1" lining extension in a scant ½" around the chasuble perimeter, then press the remaining ½" over the chasuble edge. Pin. Blind stitch in place, easing where necessary.

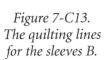

Figure 7-C13. The quilting lines for the sleeves B.

Finishing the Neckline

15. Baste the chasuble and lining layers together near the marked neck opening. Following the marked neck line on the lining, cut the neck opening from the chasuble top and lining.
16. Complete the cowl collar in the same manner described in chapter 6, steps 18 through 24 (page 64), substituting fabric B for piece I and fabric C for piece J.

A TAPERED STOLE

Sizing

Adjust the length of the stole by lengthening or shorting the piece cut from fabric A.

Prepare the Yardage

You will cut and piece several fabrics together and then cut the pieced unit lengthwise to make two identical strips before cutting out the pattern.

1. Cut the following:

Fabric	Section	Quantity	Size
A	a	one	44" x 12"
B	a	one	2½" x 12"
B	b	one	6" x 12"
C	a	two	1½" x 12"
C	b	one	4" x 12"

2. Using ¼" seams, with right sides together, piece the cut sections in the following order: Aa to one of the Ca pieces, Ba to the other Ca piece, Bb to Cb. Then join the remaining long cut edge of Ca (pieced to Aa) to Ba, and the other Ca edge to Cb. You now have a single unit piece, Aa-Ca-Ba-Ca-Bb-Cb (Figure 7-S2). Press all of the seams toward Cb.

3. Cut unit Aa-Ca-Ba-Ca-Bb-Cb in half lengthwise to make two 6" by 57" strips.

Cut the Pattern

4. Draft the stole pattern from chapter 6 (page 66) following the general instructions, page 50.

5. Wrong sides together, lay the two strips Aa-Ca-Ba-Ca-Bb-Cb so that the piecing matches exactly (flower head pins are helpful to hold fabric in place). Overlay the stole pattern with the bottom edge of the stole pattern flush with the bottom edges of Cb. Cut out following the stole pattern lines (see Figure 6-S5, page 66).

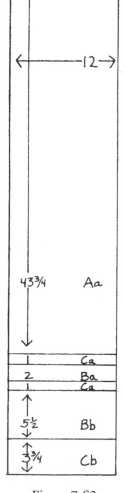

Figure 7-S2.
Piecing for the stole.

Making the Stole

6. Remove the pattern and pin sections Aa together at the neck edge to make one continuous piece. Stitch using a ½" seam. Press the seam open.

7. If a "kissing cross" is desired, work one in cross-stitch (see Chapter 6, step 7 on page 66) or another embroidery stitch, in contrasting embroidery floss.

8. Using the stole pattern, cut the stole lining from fabric C and cut the interfacing. Attach the interfacing to the facing following the general instructions, page 48. Stitch the neck seam. Press the seam open.

9. Complete the stole by hand or by machine, following the general stole instructions on page 51.

A TAPERED MANIPLE

Prepare the Yardage

You will cut and piece several fabrics together before cutting out the pattern.

1. Cut the following:

Fabric	Section	Quantity	Size
A	b	one	18" x 6"
B	c	one	2" x 12"
B	d	one	4½" x 12"
C	c	two	1½" x 12"
C	d	one	4" x 12"

2. Using ¼" seams and with right sides together, piece one of the Cc pieces to Bc and the other Cc to Bd. Then join Bc to the Cc that is joined to Bd, and the remaining edge of Bd to Cd. You now have unit Cc-Bc-Cc-Bd-Cd (Figure 7-M2). Press all the seams toward Cd.

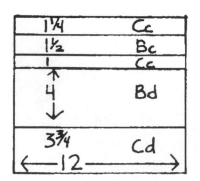

Figure 7-M2.
Initial piecing for the maniple.

3. Cut the unit Cc-Bc-Cc-Bd-Cd in half lengthwise to make two 6" by 11½" strips. Join one of the 6" ends of Cc to Ab. Repeat using the other end of Ab and the remaining Cc end. You now have a single piece, Cd-Bd-Cc-Bc-Cc-Ab-Cc-Bc-Cc-Bd-Cd (Figure 7-M3). Press the seams in the same direction as the other seams.

Cut the Pattern

4. Draft the maniple pattern from chapter 6 (page 67) following the general instructions, page 50.
5. Fold Cd-Bd-Cc-Bc-Cc-Ab-Cc-Bc-Cc-Bd-Cd in half crosswise so that the piecing matches exactly (use flower head pins to hold fabric in place). Overlay the maniple pattern with the top folded edge of the maniple pattern flush with the folded edge of Ab (see Figure 6-M5, page 67). Cut out maniple following the pattern lines.

Figure 7-M3.
Completed piecing
for the maniple.

Making the Maniple

6. Using the maniple pattern, cut the maniple lining from fabric C folded in half crosswise. Cut the inner lining from the lightweight interfacing. Attach the interlining to the facing following the general instructions, page 48.
7. Complete the maniple by hand or by machine, following general maniple instructions on page 51.

A WESTERN DEACON'S STOLE

Sizing

Sizing directions are in chapter 6 on page 67. To adjust the actual length of this stole, reduce or lengthen piece Ac. If the bottom section of the stole needs lengthening or shortening, adjust piece Ad.

Prepare the Yardage

You will cut and piece several fabrics together and then cut the pieced unit lengthwise to make two identical strips before cutting out pattern section 2. Section 1 is cut from one fabric length, piece Ac.

1. Cut the following:

Fabric	Section	Quantity	Size
A	c	one	50" x 5½"
A	d	one	15" x 11"
B	e	one	2½" x 11"
B	f	one	6" x 11"
C	e	two	1½" x 11"
C	f	one	4" x 11"

2. Using ¼" seams, and with right sides together, piece the cut sections in the following order: Ad to one of the Ce pieces, Be to the other Ce, and Bf to Cf. Then join the remaining edge of the Ce connected to Ad to Be and the remaining Be edge to Bf. You now have a single piece, Ad-Ce-Be-Ce-Bf-Cf (Figure 7-D2). Press the seams toward Cf.
3. Cut the joined pieces Ad-Ce-Be-Ce-Bf-Cf in half lengthwise to make two 5½" by 28" strips.

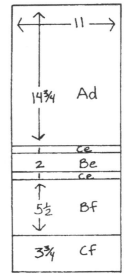

Figure 7-D2.
The piecing for
section 2 of the
deacon's stole.

Cut the Pattern

4. Draft the deacon's stole from pattern 6 (page 69) following the general instructions on page 50.
5. Overlay the sash, section 1 of the stole pattern, on the folded crosswise piece Ac, matching the fold line to the folded edge. The width should match exactly. Cut the bottom edge at its angle. Mark a dot for matching to section 2 and for the ribbon placement. Using the same pattern piece cut out the lining from fabric C and mark the dot. Cut the inner lining from the lightweight interfacing. Trim ¼" around perimeter of the interfacing.
6. Wrong sides together, align strips Ad-Ce-Be-Ce-Bf-Cf so that the piecing matches exactly (flower

head pins are helpful here). Overlay pattern section 2, keeping the bottom edges flush. Cut the top angled edge. Mark the dot for matching to section 1. Using the same pattern piece, cut the lining from fabric C and mark the dot. Cut the inner lining from lightweight interfacing. Trim ¼" around perimeter of the interfacing.

Making the Deacon's Stole

7. Attach the interfacing sections to the facing following the general instructions, page 48.
8. Complete the stole following the general instructions for the deacon's stole, pages 51–52.

A SIMPLE BURSE

Prepare the Yardage

You will cut and piece narrow strips of fabric to "frame" a fabric square for the burse top.
1. Cut the following:

Fabric	Quantity	Size
A	two	8½" squares
B	two	10" squares
C	four	1¼" x 8½"
C	four	1¼" x 10"

2. Using ¼" seams, stitch the 1¼" by 8½" C strips to the two opposing edges of each square A (Figure 7-B2). Press the seams toward A.
3. Using ¼" seams, stitch the 1¼" by 10" C strips to the two remaining cut edges of each A square (Figure 7-B3). Press the seams toward C. You now have two 10" squares for the burse covers.

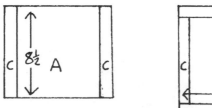 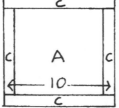

Figures 7-B2 and B3.
The placement of strips C on each square A.

Making the Burse

4. Finish the burse according to the general instructions on page 52. Use the B fabric squares for the lining.

A SIMPLE CHALICE VEIL

Prepare the Yardage

You will cut and piece several fabrics together to make the square top.
1. Cut the following:

Fabric	Section	Quantity	Size
A	d	one	10" x 23"
B	g	two	6" x 23"
C	g	four	1½" x 23"
C	h	two	1½" x 25"
C	i	one	25" square

2. Using ¼" seams and with right sides together, join two of the Cg strips to the opposing 23" edges of Ad. Then stitch the two Bg pieces to the Cg strips. Attach the remaining two Cg strips to the Bg pieces. You now have a single piece, Cg-Bg-Cg-Ad-Cg-Bg-Cg, which measures 25" by 23" (see Figure 7-V3). Press all the seams in the same direction.
3. Using ¼" seams, attach one strip Ch across one edge of Cg-Bg-Cg-Ad-Cg-Bg-Cg. Repeat on the other remaining edge. Press the seams toward the strips Ch. You now have a 25" square for the chalice veil top (Figure 7-V3).

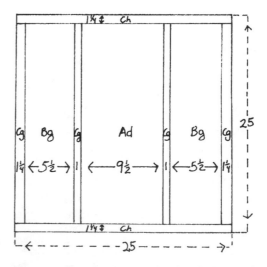

Figure 7-V3. The piecing for the chalice veil.

Making the Chalice Veil

4. Finish the chalice veil according to the general instructions, page 53. Use piece Ci for the lining. After finishing the chalice veil, lightly quilt along the two inner seams where Bg is joined to Cg.

NOTES

8.
A TRADITIONAL CHRISTMAS

∽

And the Word became flesh and lived among us . . . full of grace and truth.

—John 1:14

Christmas is a time to celebrate God becoming human. Emmanuel literally means "God with us." God's saving love is embodied in Jesus, who is fully human and fully divine. The Christmas cycle, which includes Advent, Christmas, and Epiphany, encourages us to be appreciative of God's nearness and overflowing love for us.

White vestments are worn for the feasts of the twelve days of Christmas, Epiphany, the Baptism (the first Sunday after Epiphany) and the Transfiguration (the last Sunday after Epiphany). Christmas celebrates traditions, so the pattern in this chapter incorporates enduring and traditional chasuble details: white wool, the flower ornament, and the pillar and Y-cross orphreys. White wool was the common fabric of the earliest chasubles, and the pillar orphrey was introduced early on to conceal seams. The flower ornament was one of the first nonutilitarian adornments; by the twelfth century it was replaced by or incorporated with the Y cross. Using the Y cross and flower on the back and the pillar on the front continues to be a popular way to adorn chasubles year round and worldwide.

The Byzantine or Eastern-style deacon's stole has retained its ancient name, *orarium*, in the East. The modern version is far longer than the original prototype, however. Rather than being made from a single length of cloth, it is made from two sections. The sash across the body and the tails that hang from the left shoulder create a well groomed, fitted style.

The orphreys on the chasuble and stole in this chapter reflect a Christmas motif with crowns, Christmas roses, and stars. The golden crown symbolizes the sovereignty of Christ. Many crowns symbolize the Magi, who represent the peoples of all nations, ever welcome at Christ's table. The Christmas rose, *helleborus niger*, is the ancient symbol of the Nativity, since it survives the ravages of winter and blooms at Christmastime, just as Jesus is the flower from the root of Jesse (Isaiah 11:1). The five-pointed star reminds us that Christ is the light of the world and its messianic king (compare Numbers 24:17 and Revelation 22:16) whose brightness never fades as it guides its followers through the rough waters of faithful discipleship.

The sacred monogram *ihs* is added to the central flower on the back of the chasuble. *IHS* stands for the name of Jesus in Greek (IHCUC), or *iota, eta, sigma*. January 1, the octave of Christmas, is the Feast of the Holy Name of Jesus, according to the Gospel of Luke 2:21: "After eight days had passed, it was time to circumcise the child; and he was called Jesus." Latin words have since been appended to the monogram to expand its meaning, *Ieusus Hominum Salvator* (Jesus, Savior of Humanity).

The orphreys are made up in short sections that are joined after the adornments are applied. The freezer-paper method of hand appliqué is used for all of the symbols except the *ihs*, which is machine appliquéd.

FABRIC REQUIREMENTS

Chasuble (55" wide by 52" long in front and 54" in back, finished)

Chasuble fabric, white wool: 3 yards of at least 56" width, or 6 yards of 44" width.

Orphrey fabric, deep blue silk: ⅞ yard of 44" width, or ⅔ of at least 56" width.

Lining, gold satin: 3 yards of at least 56" width, or 6 yards of 44" width.

Crowns and stars, gold silk: ½ yard.

Rose petals, white silk: ⅓ yard.

Rose centers, red cotton with metallic gold dots or red silk: ⅛ yard.

Batiste or other sheer interlining: ¾ yard.

Sulky Totally Stable© or other removable machine appliqué stabilizer: a 4" by 5" scrap.

Deacon's Stole (5" wide, 46" girth, and 44" tails, finished)

White wool: ¾ yard of 44", or ⅓ yard of 54".

Deep blue for appliqué base: ⅔ yard.

Lining, gold satin: 1⅓ yards of 44", or ⅔ yard of 54".

Crowns and stars, gold silk: ⅓ yard.

Rose petals, white silk: ¼ yard.

Rose centers, red cotton with metallic gold dots or red silk: ⅛ yard.

Batiste or other sheer interlining: ¾ yard.

Non-fusible, light to midweight interfacing: 1½ yards.

Velcro™ dots: two sets.

Notions (beyond the general supply list on pages 45–46)

Waxed freezer paper such as Reynolds brand.

Tear-away stabilizer: at least ¼ yard for each project.

Clear template plastic: two sheets for the chasuble and stole, or one sheet for the stole.

Tweezers for pulling out the waxed paper and the basting threads.

Aleene's® Tacky Glue to hold wayward threads in place.

Long thin needles for hand appliqué (milliner's size 10 or 11 works well).

Basting thread.

Accent thread a shade darker than the gold crown fabric; Sulky Rayon is a good choice.

A Gothic Chasuble with Orphreys

Sizing

These directions are for a medium Gothic chasuble with tapered shoulders. Make size adjustments when you draft the pattern. Reduce or lengthen the orphrey background fabric that is left plain at the top and bottom ends or, if necessary, adjust the space between the symbols.

Draft and Cut the Pattern

1. Draft chasuble pattern 8 following the general instructions on page 50.

2. Cut the chasuble and chasuble lining from the drafted pattern, being sure that the centers are along the lengthwise fold of the fabric. On the chasuble pieces, lightly mark the center front and back lines from neck to hem.

3. If you need to piece your fabric, open out the lengthwise fold, fold over crosswise, and align the centers along the doubled selvage edges with the selvage trimmed off. Add a ½" seam allowance along the centers (Figure 8-C3). Using a ½" seam, with wrong sides together, stitch the center seams of the chasuble, front and back. Press open. Use the seam line as the center line. With right sides together, stitch the center seams of the lining, front and back. Press open.

4. On the chasuble front and back, measure and draw a line 2" parallel and to the left of the center lines. On the chasuble back, measure over 8½" from the center line along both shoulder lines. This marks the placement line of the Y orphreys. If the person who will wear the chasuble is available, check the measurement from the nape of the neck to the top of the shoulder and add ½". Use that measurement rather than the average 8½". Measure down 10½" from the center of the neck line. Draw a line connecting the shoulder mark to the center back mark (Figure 8-C4). If you altered the shoulder line, you may need to adjust the center back mark. Aim for a pleasing angle from the shoulders to the center back—this line falls ½" below the seam line of the inside edge of the Y orphreys. Set chasuble and lining aside.

The Orphreys

You will make plastic templates of the crowns, roses, and stars and then trace the template patterns onto waxed freezer paper. After cutting out the paper templates, you will iron them onto the wrong side of the appliqué fabrics. Then you will add a seam allowance, cut out the shapes, and appliqué them in place. Once the orphreys are adorned, they will be stitched onto the chasuble top.

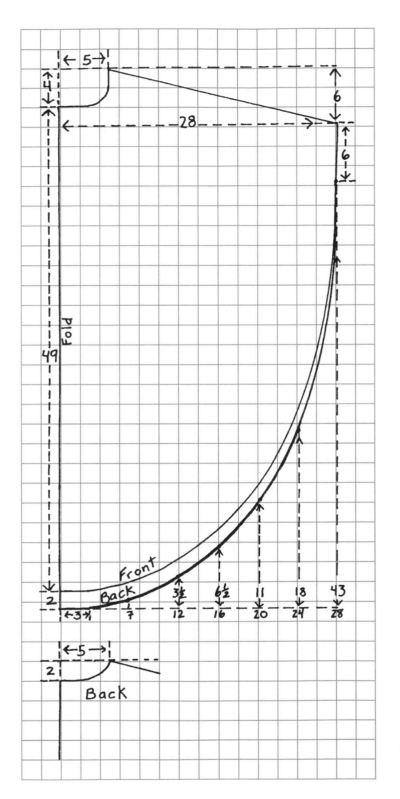

Pattern 8. Gothic (medium) chasuble with tapered shoulders, rounded front and neckline. Back neckline is shown separately below chasuble. Cut one front and one back from fabric and lining. Scale: one square = 2 inches.

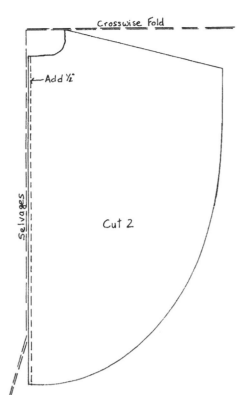

Figure 8-C3. Cutting the chasuble from a narrow-width fabric. Addition of a ½" seam allowance required down the center front.

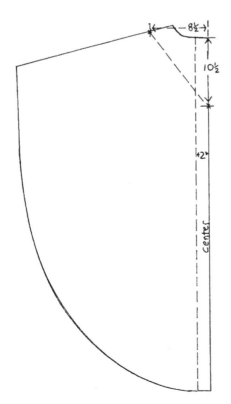

Figure 8-C4. Drafting the back orphrey placement lines.

Hand Appliqué Tips

- Baste with a contrasting color so that the thread is easy to see when you need to remove it.
- Appliqué with a long thin needle (milliner's 10 or 11) and close-matching thread.
- Keep your stitches spaced about ⅟16" apart.
- Use your needle to push under protruding threads and fabric, hold in place with your free thumb, and stitch to hold.
- Wayward threads that resist the needle turn may be tucked in place with Aleene's® Tacky Glue. Put a dab of glue on the end of a pin and gently push the thread under with the glued point.
- Give your thread a gentle tug after each stitch to stabilize the stitch and to force the thread under the fabric.
- Use round-tipped tweezers to remove the basting thread and the freezer paper.

5. The rose and crown patterns are their finished size without the seam allowance. To make these patterns easier to work with, you may want to copy them and then make a mirror copy of each pattern. Tape them together to make a complete image without the fold. Trace the complete central flower, the small rose, and the crown—including its accent lines—onto the template plastic. Use these templates for placement guides. Carefully cut exactly on the lines of the crown.

6. Onto template plastic, trace—from the large and small roses—the rose petal with the * and small horizontal mark along one edge, and one star point. Be sure to transfer the small petal mark (if you are left-handed, place the mark on the reverse side). Trace the center star from the large rose and the circle from the small rose. Cut each petal, point, and center exactly on the traced lines.

7. On the unwaxed side of the freezer paper, using the template patterns, trace five large rose petals, five large star points, one center star, six crowns, forty small rose petals, forty small star points, and eight center circles. Cut out exactly on the traced lines. On each petal, transfer the small line on the rose petals.

8. Cut out a 10¾" diameter circle (use a compass or the provided pattern plus a ⅜" seam allowance) from the remaining gold silk. Set your iron on the silk setting. On the wrong side of the remnant gold silk, iron the freezer paper star points and crowns,

Figure 8-C8. After ironing freezer paper to the wrong side of the fabric, add a ⅜" seam allowance.

leaving enough fabric around each pattern to allow for a ⅜" seam allowance around the perimeter of each appliqué piece. Orient the crowns and points with the obvious grain of the silk to suggest a radiance emanating from the pieces. Mark a ⅜" seam allowance around each pattern and cut each piece out along the seam allowance line (Figure 8-C8).

9. Iron the rose petals to the wrong side of the white silk, allowing for a ⅜" seam allowance around each petal. Orient the petals with the grain of the silk to suggest veins running through the petals. Cut the petals from the fabric, adding a ⅜" seam allowance (see Figure 8-C8).

10. Iron the center star and the center circles onto the wrong side of the red fabric, accommodating for the seam allowance. Cut the shapes from the fabric, adding a ⅜" seam allowance (see Figure 8-C8).

11. From the blue silk and the batiste interlining, cut the following (see cutting layout in Figure 8-C11—you do not need to cut out a batiste circle):

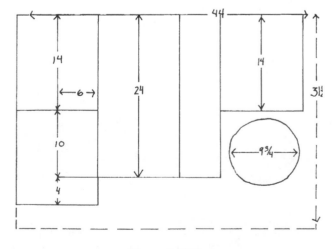

Figure 8-C11.
Cutting layout for the orphreys and the flower.

Quantity	Size
one	9¾" diameter circle (use a compass or the provided pattern plus a ⅜" seam allowance)
three	6" x 24" strips
five	6" x 14" strips
one	6" x 10" strip
one	6" x 4" strip

Using a zigzag stitch and with wrong sides together, attach the identical silk pieces to the batiste pieces along all four edges. This will stabilize and strengthen the silk and finish the edges so they do not ravel while you are working.

12. Clip the seam allowance of the inside corners and curves of the crowns, stopping at the freezer paper. Using the freezer paper as your guide, press (with an iron or your finger) the ⅜" seam allowance over the freezer paper to the inside of each crown, beginning at an inside corner. Mitre the points by folding horizontally across the top of each point, then folding in the sides for a smooth, sharp point (Figure 8-C12). Baste the folded-over seam allowance in place. Transfer the accent lines from the template to the right side of each crown.

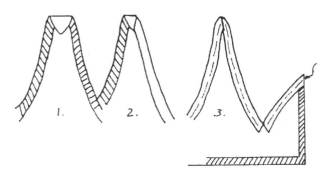

Figure 8-C12. To make a clean point:
1. press tip of seam allowance down; 2. fold in one side;
3. then the other side; 4. to turn in at the "valley"
points; snip to the freezer paper.

13. Apply one of the crowns to one of the 6" by 24" blue strips, and the rest of the crowns to the five 6" by 14" blue strips. Right sides out, place the bottom raw edge of each crown ⅛" above the bottom edge of each strip, centering the sides to within ⅛" of the side edges (Figure 8-C13). Baste the side edges but leave the bottom open so that the paper can be removed. Blind stitch the folded edges of the crowns in place, being careful to run the needle just inside the folds without catching

the freezer paper. After stitching the crowns in place, remove the basting thread, reach between the bottom edge of the crown and blue strip, loosen the freezer paper, and pull it out. Baste the bottom edge closed. Using your machine threaded with a darker gold color, satin stitch the two accent lines at the base of each crown (see chapter 10, machine appliqué tips, page 117). Use tear-away stabilizer under the blue strip to stabilize the stitching. Set the "crowned" 6" by 24" strip aside.

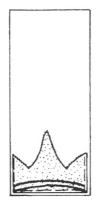

Figure 8-C13. Placement of crown at base of orphrey strip.

14. Lay the small rose plastic template with the bottom edge of the rose 2" above a finished crown and 2½" below the top raw edge on one of the 6" by 14" blue strips. Have the top star point centered upward. Lightly mark the placement of the rose petals. Mark the remaining 6" by 14" blue strips. On the 6" by 10" blue strip, mark the rose with its top edge 2½" below the top edge of the strip. The two small roses above the flower will be worked later.

15. Clip the seam allowance of the inner curves and the horizontal mark of the rose petals and press in the seam allowance of the petals, in the same manner as the crowns. Leave the bottom edge and the side below the small mark unfolded (Figure 8-C15). Baste the folded seam allowance in place. If you are left-handed, reverse the side that is kept unfolded and work in the opposite direction shown in Figure 8-C16.

Figure 8-C15. Clip the inside curves and at the *, then press under the seam allowance of petal except at the bottom and below the horizontal mark.

Figure 8-C16. To appliqué the rose, begin at the junction of two petals; at the overlap of petals, pull the top petal away and baste under petal.

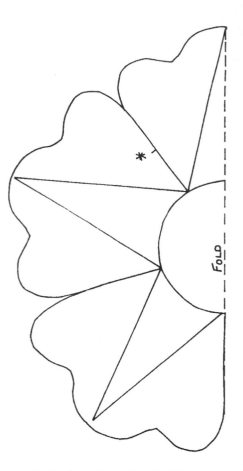

Pattern 8. Orphrey Rose. One half in actual size.

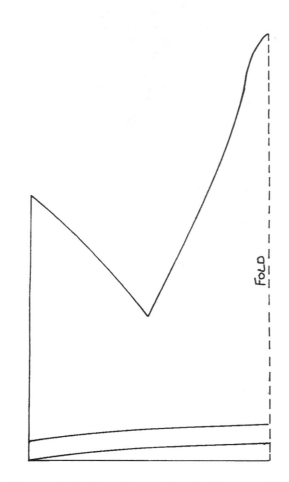

Pattern 8. Orphrey Crown. One half in actual size.

16. Guided by your marks and the template plastic, arrange the petals on the marked strips above the crowns so that a folded petal edge overlaps an unfolded edge. Notice the arrangement of the petals relative to the star. Be sure to place the petals so that the star will be centered and upright. Pin in place. Blind stitch one petal, beginning with the top petal at the intersection of two petals and at the end, pull away the adjacent top petal to baste down the under petal (Figure 8-C16). Remove the basting and freezer paper. Working around the circle, blind stitch the whole of each petal, removing the basting and freezer paper as each petal is completed. When you complete the circle, blind stitch the remaining edge of the initial petal in place.

17. Press and baste the seam allowance of the star points in the same manner as the crowns and petals. Leave the bottom edge open. Using the complete rose template as a guide, pin the star points in place over the roses. Blind stitch them in place, then remove the basting and freezer paper.

18. Beginning and ending on the wrong side of the fabric, run a hand-basting stitch ⅛" in along the cut edge of the red circle centers. Pull up the end threads of the basting to gather the seam allowance of the circles inward until a circle guided by the freezer paper is formed. Tie off the threads to hold the turned seam allowance and remove the paper. Center the circles over the raw edges of the star points and petals. Blind stitch in place.

19. With right sides together, align the bottom edge (with a crown) of a 6" by 14" strip to the top edge (no crown) of another 6" by 14" strip. Pin. Stitch across the matched edges using a ½" seam, being sure to catch in the raw edge of the crown. Press the seam away from the crown. To the top edge, above the rose, add the 6" by 24" strip adorned with a single crown at its bottom edge. To the bottom of these joined strips, add the unadorned 6" by 4" strip. You now have the orphrey for the chasuble back.

20. Repeat the process, joining the remaining three 6" by 14" strips. At the bottom of the joined strips,

Monogram Pattern 8. The ihs *pattern with centering lines for the flower in actual size.*

add the 6" by 10" strip that is adorned with a rose. This completes the front orphrey; it should look like the drawing at the beginning of the chapter.

The Flower

21. Stay stitch a scant ⅜" from the cut edge around the 9¾" blue and 10¾" gold circles. Beginning and ending on the wrong side of the fabric, hand baste close to the cut edge of both circles. Pull up the ends of the basting thread to lightly gather and turn in the ⅜" seam allowances—use the stay-stitching as your guide. Press the seam allowances under. Set the gold circle aside.

22. Following steps 15–17 above, appliqué the rose petals and star just within the folded edge of the blue circle. Clip the inside corners of the center red star and press the ⅜" seam allowance to the inside over the freezer paper. Press in the points as directed in step 12. Place the center star so that its points meet where the points of the gold star intersect (refer to your template). Blind stitch in place. When you are about ½" from closing the star, reach in the opening with tweezers to pull out the freezer paper. Continue stitching the star closed. Mark the center point of the star.

23. Trace the *ihs* monogram onto the paper side of the Totally Stable© appliqué stabilizer. Press the stabilizer onto the right side of a 4" by 5" scrap of the blue silk. Cut out the stabilized fabric exactly along the stabilizer pattern. Center the mono-

gram over the completed flower by matching the intersection of the centering lines on the template with the marked center on the star. Be sure the monogram sits straight; use the top arms of the large star as a guide. Pin, then baste in place. Machine appliqué the monogram following the instructions in chapter 10 on page 117, omitting the slash in the "s." Carefully tear away the stabilizer with tweezers. Then satin stitch the slash through the "s." Use a tear-away stabilizer under the flower to stabilize while stitching and tear it away after all of the stitching is completed.

24. Center the adorned blue circle over the gold circle. Pin. Blind stitch in place.

Adorning the Chasuble

25. Stay stitch a scant ½" along the lengthwise edges of the completed orphreys. Wrong side up, turn under the left lengthwise edge ½". Right side up, smooth the chasuble front on a large flat surface. Right sides together, align the unfolded edge of the front orphrey along the line drawn 2" parallel to the center line. Be sure the orphrey is in the correct directional orientation, that its top edge is even with the cut neckline, and that the folded edge extends toward the sleeve, not toward the center (Figure 8-C25). Pin and baste. Stitch in a ½" seam. Press the orphrey over the center of the chasuble. Baste, then blind stitch the folded edge in place.

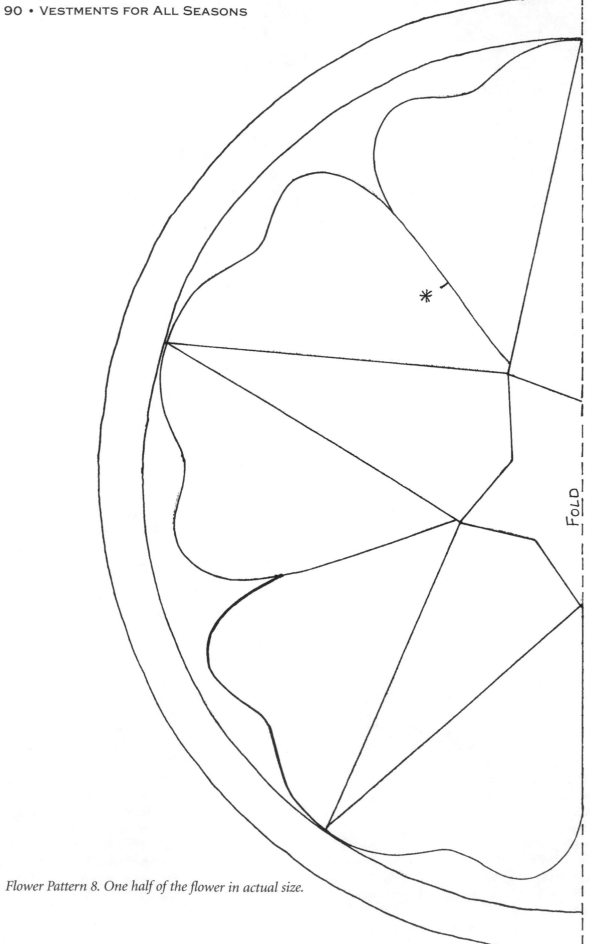

Flower Pattern 8. One half of the flower in actual size.

FOLD

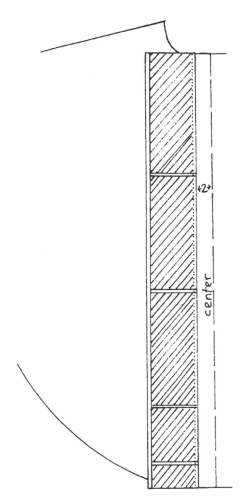

Figure 8-C25. Align the pieced orphrey, right sides together, along the placement line 2" to the left of the chasuble center.

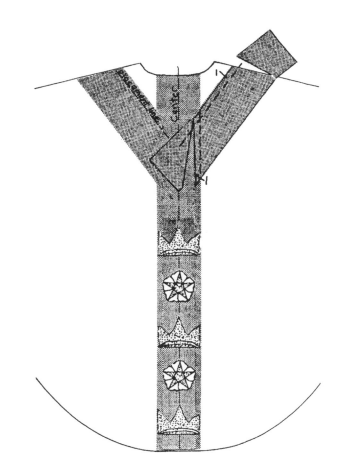

Figure 8-C26. Cut the "Y" orphreys to size by laying out on the chasuble back. Place the inside length of the orphrey 1" above the placement line and add 1" beyond the intersection of the Y with the center orphrey.

26. Right side up, smooth the chasuble back on a large flat surface. Center the back orphrey right side up on the chasuble, beginning at the neck edge and extending to the hem. Lay the two unadorned 6" by 24" strips in a Y, having the inside raw edges extend 1" beyond the placement lines. Draw the shoulder line across the top edge of the strips, and draw the intersecting lines with the outer edges of the center orphrey toward the bottom edges. Trim the bottom angle 1" beyond the drawn line and exactly along the shoulder lines (Figure 8-C26). Lay the flower over the orphrey intersection. The ½" seam allowance of the orphreys will show beyond the flower.

27. Using the small rose template, position the roses on the Y orphreys so that the bottom edge of the rose is about 2" above the seamed edge of the flower. Have the stars point toward the shoulder top to accentuate the Y. Lightly mark their placement.

Remove the Y orphreys and appliqué the roses where marked, following the instructions in steps 16-18.

28. Press the longest edge of the Y orphreys under ½". With right sides together, align the remaining lengthwise raw edge of the Y orphreys along the placement lines drawn on the chasuble back, having the pressed edges of the orphreys toward the chasuble center and the shoulder edges matched at the ½" seam junction (Figure 8-C28). Stitch the orphreys to the chasuble in a ½" seam. Press the orphreys to their right-side-out position. Baste the ends in place. Baste then blind stitch the folded edges.

29. Right side up, smooth the chasuble back on a large flat surface. Apply the center back orphrey as instructed for the front orphrey in step 25.

30. Center the flower over the intersecting orphreys. Pin, baste, and blind stitch in place.

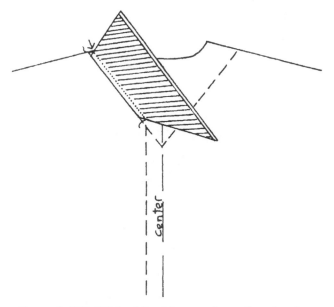

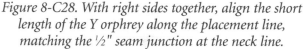

Figure 8-C28. With right sides together, align the short length of the Y orphrey along the placement line, matching the ½" seam junction at the neck line.

Completing the chasuble:

31. Right sides together, align the chasuble shoulder edges. Pin and stitch the shoulder seams in a ½" seam. Press the seams open. Stitch the shoulder seams of the lining.

32. Stay stitch the neck edges of the chasuble and the lining. With right sides together, smooth the chasuble over the lining, matching shoulder seams and centers. Pin the outer edge all the way around, front and back. Baste.

33. Turn the chasuble right side out by pulling it through the neck opening. Lightly baste the lining to the chasuble along the neck edge. Press the outside edges and hang the chasuble on a padded hanger for a few days. After the chasuble has relaxed, check to see if the lining hangs smoothly without puckers or sagging. If the hang is suitable, remove the neck basting, turn the chasuble inside out (right sides together), and stitch the outer edge, where basted, in a ½" seam. Clip curves, turn, and press. If the lining puckers or sags, remove the hem basting at the problem areas, adjust the lining to fit, and tack in place. Once satisfied, continue as directed above.

34. Finish the neck edge by turning the chasuble and lining under ½" all around (the chasuble seam allowance is folded inward toward the lining and the lining seam allowance is folded inward toward the chasuble), clipping where necessary within the stay-stitching to make a smooth fold. The chasuble and lining folded edges should meet neatly. Baste, then blind stitch closed. If desired, topstitch the neck and outside edges ¼" in from the finished seams.

A BYZANTINE DEACON'S STOLE

Sizing

Adjust the length of the stole by lengthening or shortening the pattern. The sash should fit smoothly over the chest and under the arm. The tails should hang to just below the knees.

Preparing the Stole

You will cut the stole fabric lengths, and then apply the crowns, roses, and stars to the stole tail pieces as directed. Then you will finish sewing the pieces together to complete the stole.

1. Draft the deacon's stole pattern 8, following the instructions on page 50. With each fabric folded in half, wrong sides together, cut the front and back sash pieces and the two tails from the lining and the interfacing. Be sure to transfer the dots and "x" to the right side of the lining. Attach the interfacing to the lining following the general instructions on page 48.

2. With the white wool folded in half, cut the front and back sash pieces and transfer the dot. Cut two white wool pieces, 6" square. An easy way to adjust the length of the stole tails is to lengthen or shorten this small piece.

3. From the blue silk and the batiste interlining, cut six 6" by 14" strips. Using a zigzag stitch and with wrong sides together, attach the identical silk pieces to the batiste pieces along all four edges. This will stabilize and strengthen the silk and finish the edges so they don't ravel while you are working.

4. Following the chasuble steps 5–7 above, make your pattern templates and trace the following onto freezer paper: six crowns, thirty small rose petals, thirty small star points, and six center circles.

5. From the gold, white, and red adornment fabric, cut the star points, the rose petals, and the centers as instructed in the chasuble steps 8–10 above (omit the large circle).

6. Prepare the crowns following chasuble step 12. Appliqué the six crowns at the base of the 6" by 14" blue strips, following chasuble step 13.

7. Prepare and appliqué the roses, stars, and centers as instructed in chasuble steps 14–18.

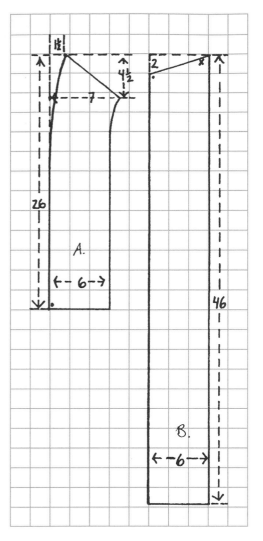

Pattern 8. Deacon's Stole.
Byzantine style in two parts, A. sash and B. tail.
Cut two of each from fabric, lining and interfacing.
Scale: one square = 2 inches.

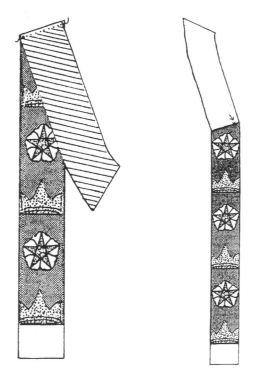

Figure 8-D10.
Match the dots of the
stole sash to tail.

Figure 8-D11.
The placement of the loop
side of Velcro™ on the stole
seam between the front
sash and back tail.

tail pattern and trim the tails along the top and bottom edges. Transfer the dot.

Making the Stole

10. With right sides together, pin the stole sash to the tail, matching the dots (Figure 8-D10). Stitch in a ½" seam. Do the same with the lining. Press the seams open.

11. Place the hook side of the Velcro™ dots over the "x" or centered on the seam line and 1" in from the raw edge on the right side of both lining sections. On the right side of the stole seam that joins the front sash to the back tail, place a loop side of Velcro™. The front sash can be determined by holding the stole to your body—the front extends from the right hip to the left shoulder, forcing the tail down the back—or compare with Figure 8-D11. Stitch the Velcro™ in place.

12. With right sides together, pin the center sash seams of the stole and the lining. Stitch in a ½" seam, stop stitching, and backstitch ½" short of the top (the short side) edge to ease the inside "V" turn; press the seams open.

8. Right sides together, align the bottom edge (with a crown) of a 6" by 14" strip to the top edge (no crown) of another 6" by 14" strip. Pin. Stitch across the matched edges in a ½" seam, being sure to catch in the raw edge of the crown. Press the seam away from the crown. Add a third 6" by 14" strip to the two joined strips in the same manner. You should have two identical stole tails measuring 40" long.

9. To the bottom of each pieced stole tail, add the 6" square piece of white wool using a ½" seam. The completed stole tails should look like the drawing on the chapter divider. Wrong sides together, align the two stole tails exactly, then overlay the stole

13. Right sides together, lay the stole over the lining, matching the seams. Pin the complete outside edge. Beginning at a long edge of the sash, stitch the outer edge of the stole to the lining in a ½" seam, pivoting at the corners and stopping 6" from the starting point. Trim the corners, clip the sash curves, and grade the seams. Turn the stole right side out by pulling it through the 6" opening. Use the point turner to force out clean corners. Press the edges. Blind stitch the opening closed.

14. Wear the stole by placing the center sash seam under the right arm. Hang the tail connected to the front of the sash down the back. Pull the tail connected to the back sash to the front, hooking the Velcro™ together to hold the tails at the shoulder. The extra Velcro™ piece should be against the clothing to reduce slippage.

NOTES

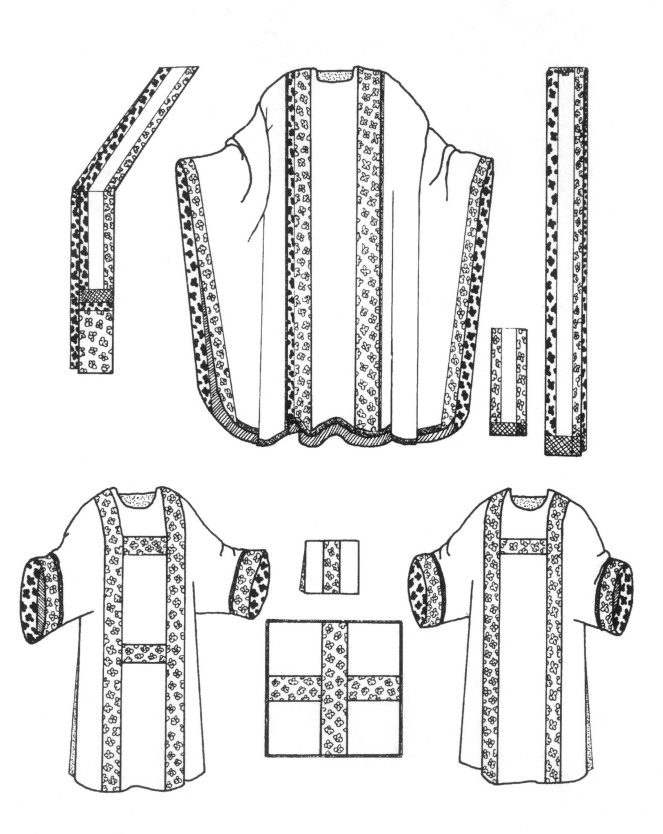

9.
Lent: An Early Church
Basic for the High Mass Set

~

Rend your hearts and not your clothing; turn back to the Lord,
your God, for he is gracious and merciful, slow to anger, and
abounding in steadfast love.

—Joel 2:13

Lent centers on repentance and renewal; it's a time to prepare for the celebration of Christ's passion, death, and resurrection. The liturgy focuses on the days Jesus spent in the wilderness, while in our own lives we try to emphasize honesty and humility. We are invited to follow Christ by turning from sin and indifference, and to practice sincerity and resolve. We are charged to consider the temptations we have succumbed to—they lessen our ability to follow Christ.

Lent concludes with Holy Week, which commemorates the final week of Jesus' earthly ministry: his triumphal entry into Jerusalem, the Last Supper, his passion, crucifixion, death, and burial. By the grace of God, we are invited to identify with Jesus; his suffering and death was for our redemption.

The Lenten vestments in this chapter are patterned after those of the ancient church. They are made of a natural, hand-woven fabric, with violet orphreys reminiscent of the Roman *clavi* because of their color and placement. The Romans also used the orphrey width to denote the wearer's status. The orphreys are 4" wide on the chasuble, 3½" on the dalmatic, and 3" on the tunicle. A touch of black is added to emphasize the introspection of the season and to create an asymmetrical zip—a reminder of the way Lent puts us a bit off balance. Black or gray is recommended to coordinate with the violet. A violet cotton lamé is used to add a touch of gold; it gets its body from the cording trim.

Included in this pattern set are an unlined monastic chasuble, dalmatic, and tunicle. The monastic chasuble is a large rectangle with rounded corners. Rather than a full pattern, the curve at the corners is detailed. The neck opening is rounded in front, squared in back, and finished with a facing, for which a pattern is provided. The priest's stole and maniple are of a continuous width; they use the interfacing as a pattern base cut to exact size. The deacon may wear the dalmatic and the lay Eucharistic minister may wear the tunicle even if a solemn High Mass is not being celebrated. They are made from the same pattern. The deacon's stole follows the pattern from chapter 6.

The orphreys and apparels are made from cotton. If you choose to use a wide braid, omit the ½" seam allowance when you draw the placement lines, and run the braid exactly along the placement lines. If you use a heavy fabric, cut the finished orphrey and apparel to the finished width plus 1", then fold one long end under ½" and stitch the remaining cut length to the garments in the same manner as the doubled-over cotton.

Fabric Requirements

Chasuble (60" wide by 54" long in front and 56" long in back, finished)

As long as the fabric is at least 40" wide, the yardage for the primary chasuble fabric A allows for the chasuble, stole, and maniple. To allow for the burse and chalice veil, add another ⅔ yard—⅓ yard if the width is 60". Fabric B allows for all of the pieces except the dalmatic and tunicle unless 4¼ yards are purchased. The yardage for fabrics C and D do allow for all pieces.

Fabric A, a natural hand-weave or linen: 4¾ yards of 44" width, or 3¼ yards of 60" width.

Fabric B, a violet cotton for the orphreys and sleeve border: 3¼ yards of either width.

Fabric C, a black/gray companion to fabric B: 3¼ yards of either width.

Fabric D, a violet lamé, for the cording and hem binding: 1 yard.

Fabric E, a linen coordinate for the neck facing: ⅓ yard of either width.

Interfacing: lightweight, ⅓ yard.

Cording: 6⅓ yards of ¼".

Stole (4" wide by 116" long, finished)

Fabric A: 3 ⅛ yards by 2½" wide.
Fabric B: 3 ⅛ yards by 1¾" wide.
Fabric C: 3 ⅛ yards by 5¾" wide.
Fabric D: ¼ yard.
Non-fusible, light to midweight interfacing: 1¼ yards.
Lace hem tape to match fabric D: ½ yard of ¾".

Maniple (4" wide by 38" long, finished)

Fabric A: 1 yard by 2½" wide.
Fabric B: 1 yard by 6½" wide.
Fabric C: none.
Fabric D: ¼ yard.
Non-fusible, light to midweight interfacing: 1 yard.
Lace hem tape to match fabric D: ½ yard of ¾".
Elastic: ¼ yard of ¼".

Dalmatic (45" long and 50" wide) or Tunicle (43" long and 46" wide, finished)

Fabric A, a natural hand-weave or linen: 2½ yards of at least a 44" width for one garment.

Fabric B, a violet cotton for the orphreys and sleeve border: 2½ yards of either width (allows for both the dalmatic and the tunicle).

Fabric C, a black/gray companion to fabric B: ⅞ yard of either width (allows for both garments).

Fabric D, a violet cotton lamé for the cording: ½ yard (allows for both garments).

Fabric E, a linen coordinate for the facings: ¾ yard of either width (allows for both garments).

Interfacing: lightweight, ¾ yard.

Cording: 1½ yards of ¼".

Deacon's Stole (4½" wide, 24" sash, and 27" tails, finished)

Fabric A: 1⅓ yards by 5" wide.

Fabric B: 1⅜ yards by 9" wide.
Fabric C: 1⅜ yard by 17" wide.
Fabric D: ¼ yard.
Non-fusible, light to midweight interfacing: 1⅜ yards.
One large bobby pin with rubber tips.

Burse (9" square, finished)

Fabric A: ⅓ yard.
Fabric B: ⅓ yard.
White batiste for interlining: ⅓ yard.
Plexiglas™: two thin, 9" squares.

Chalice Veil (24" square, finished)

Fabric A: ⅓ yard.
Fabric B: ¼ yard.
Fabric C: ¾ yard.
Fabric D for cording: ½ yard.
Cording, narrow: 3 yards.

A MONASTIC CHASUBLE

Sizing

The directions are for a large, monastic chasuble. Make size adjustments when cutting fabric A.

Prepare the Yardage

First cut the orphreys from fabric B for all of the vestments being made to assure that you do not cut away some of the needed orphrey length when cutting a smaller piece from B.

1. Cut the following:
   From A: If a 57" width is used, cut the length to 113", or the exact total finished length from hem to hem desired plus 3". If you are using a lesser width, cut one full length (113") plus a 57" length; then cut:

Fabric	Quantity	Size
B	one	113" x 9"
B	one	113" x 3¾"
B	two	94" by 2½"
		(or 7 - 30" by 2½" if using 44" fabric and making the dalmatic and tunicle)
C	one	113" x 5¾"
C	two	94" x 2½"
D	one	20½" x 2" (if using less than a 57" width of fabric A)
D	one	36" square for cording and hem bias strips

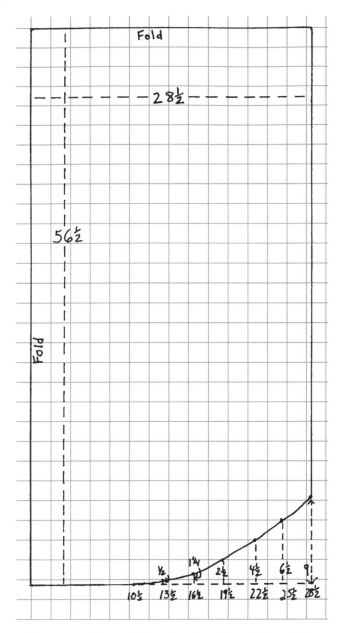

Fold

28½

56½

Fold

⅛ 1¼ 2½ 4½ 6½ 9

10½ 13½ 16½ 19½ 22½ 25½ 28½

Pattern 9. Monastic (ample) chasuble; draft neckline from facing. Scale: one square = 2 inches.

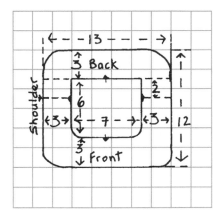

13

3 Back

Shoulder

6

3 7 3 12

2½

3 Front

Pattern 9. Neck facing for the chasuble, dalmatic, and tunicle. Scale: one square = 2 inches.

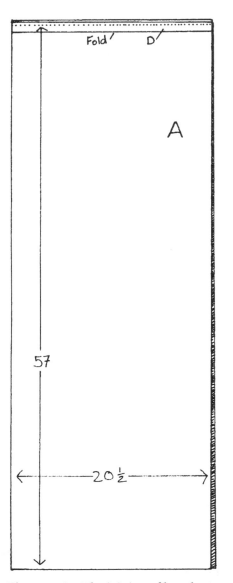

Fold   D

A

57

20½

Figure 9-C3. The joining of lengths A and enclosing in a narrow D strip.

2. If you are using at least a 57" width of fabric A, skip to step 11. Otherwise, trim off the fold of the 57" length of fabric A to a 20½" width to yield two 20½" by 57" lengths. Wrong sides together, pin the two lengths together along their 20½" width. Baste in a scant ½" seam.

3. Fold the 20½" by 2" strip cut from fabric D in half lengthwise. Press. Align the cut edges of the folded strip ⅛" from the cut edge of the basted seam of fabric A (Figure 9-C3). Pin. Stitch a ½" seam through all thicknesses. Press the folded strip D over the seam and blind stitch in place to enclose the seam.

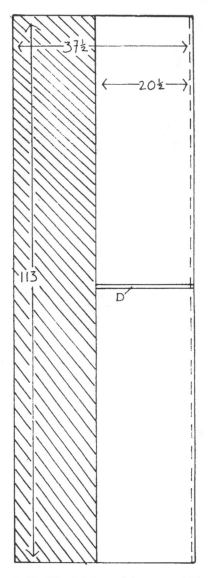

Figure 9-C4. The joining of the two widths of A, wrong sides together.

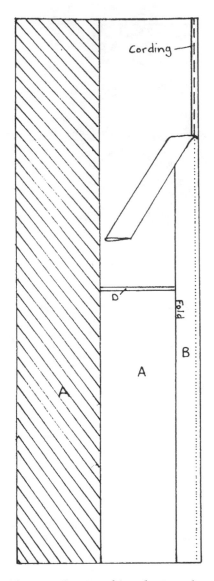

Figure 9-C6. Attaching the B orphrey in a corded seam.

4. Trim the width of the 113" length of fabric A to 37½". With wrong sides together, pin the two fabric A pieces together along their long cut edges. Baste in a scant ½" seam (Figure 9-C4).

5. Prepare the 6⅓ yards of ¼" cording from fabric D as directed in the general instructions on page 49. Align the raw edges of the cording along the raw edges of the basted chasuble seam. Be sure the narrower (20½") width of A is on top of the wider width of A, as shown in Figure 9-C6. Baste the cording in place.

6. Fold the 113" by 9" strip of fabric B in half lengthwise. Press. Pin the cut edges of this strip along the seam edge of fabric A and the cording, keeping all the cut edges flush (Figure 9-C6).

Using a zipper foot, stitch in a ½" seam. Grade seams and press the B strip toward the 37" width of A to enclose the seam and reveal the cording. Pin the folded edge of B to A. Blind stitch in place. You now have a joined and corded width of A measuring 57" wide by 113" long with both seams enclosed, one in a narrow strip of D, the other within a 4" B orphrey.

7. Make the other orphrey by stitching in a ¼" seam the length of the 113" by 3¾" strip of B to the 113" by 5¾" strip of C, right sides together. Press the seam toward B. Fold the seamed 9" width of B-C in half lengthwise. Press.

8. Smooth the pieced A on a large flat surface. Measure and draw two lines onto A: one 9½"

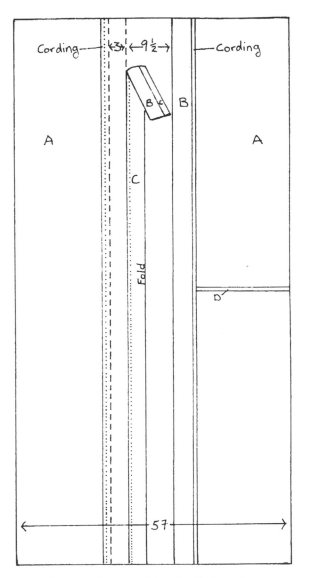

Figure 9-C8. Attaching the B-C orphrey and the second row of cording.

parallel to the folded edge of the B orphrey; the other, 12½" parallel to B or 3" from the first line. With right sides together, align the cut edges of the folded strip B-C to the first drawn line, with the fold toward the completed orphrey and the B-C seam against A (Figure 9-C8). Pin and baste in place.

9. Align the cut edges of the remaining cording along the second drawn line, with the cut edges toward the center of the chasuble and the actual cording extending just past the drawn line toward the sleeve (see Figure 9-C8). Fold the basted orphrey toward the sleeve; the folded edge should meet the rim of the cording. If not, adjust the cording position until it meets the orphrey fold.

Move the orphrey away, baste, then stitch the cording to the chasuble with a zipper foot.

10. Stitch strip B-C to A in a ½" seam. Press the folded edge of B-C away from the other orphrey to enclose the seam. Pin and blind stitch in place along the cording stitching line. You now have two corded orphreys, 9" apart. Go to step 12.

11. If you are using at least a 57" width of fabric A, prepare the B orphrey and the cording as in step 6 and make the orphrey B-C as in step 7 above. Attach the two orphreys by measuring and drawing two parallel lines—8" in from both sides of the center fold line—the complete length of the fabric (see Figure 9-DT4 and Figure 9-DT7, pages 106–107). Baste the cording along the two drawn lines, with the cording toward the sleeves and its cut edges along the placement lines as they face the chasuble center. Attach the B and B-C orphrey in the same manner described in step 6 above, pressing the folded edges of the orphreys toward the center.

Finishing the Neckline

12. Draft the neck facing pattern 9 (page 99) following the general instructions on page 50. Using the facing pattern, cut out the facing and interfacing, making outward notches at the center front, back, and shoulder lines. Attach the interfacing to the facing following the general instructions, page 48. Finish the outside edge of the facing by turning it under ¼" and stitching or by serging.

13. Fold the chasuble in half lengthwise, matching the outside edges and being sure the orphreys are in line. With pins, mark the shoulder line. The shoulder line falls at 56½" or at the midpoint from the cut 113" length; it is in line with the fabric D strip attached in step 3. Mark the center fold line 4" toward the front and 2" toward the back from the shoulder line (see Figure 9-C14).

14. Open out the chasuble and smooth it on a large flat surface with the right side up. Right sides together, lay the neck facing on the chasuble, matching the centers and the shoulder lines. Place the facing front so that the B-C orphrey is on your left, the wearer's right. Be sure that the facing is exactly centered and straight between the orphreys (Figure 9-C14). Pin and baste in place. Stitch ½" from the facing neck opening edge, pivoting at the back corners.

15. Cut the chasuble neck opening along the facing cut edge. Trim, grade, and clip the seam. Press the

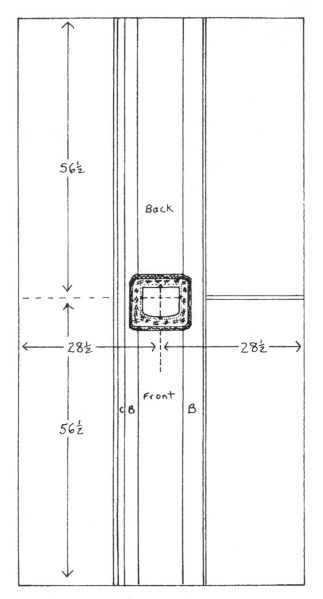

Figure 9-C14. Placement of the neck facing.

facing toward the neck opening and, keeping the
chasuble free, understitch the facing to the neckline seam allowance, breaking the stitching within
1" of the back corners (Figure 9-C15). Turn and
press facing to the inside. Tack along the sides
under the orphreys.

Finishing the Hemlines

16. Once again, lay the chasuble in half lengthwise
on a large flat surface. Make sure the orphreys
and shoulder lines are in perfect alignment. If
your fabric is wider than 57", trim both outside
edges 28½" from the center fold. On the chasuble
back, mark the bottom curved edge following

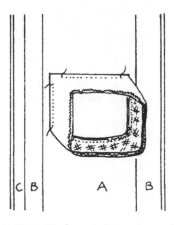

Figure 9-C15. Under stitching the neck facing.

the pattern 9 instructions (page 99). Cut along
the bottom curved edge.

17. Shorten the chasuble front by trimming 2" from
the bottom width. Mark the bottom curved edge
following the pattern 9 instructions. Cut along the
bottom curved edge.

18. Cut and join two 64" by 2" bias strips, then fold in
half lengthwise. Press. Pin the cut edges of one bias
strip along the inside of the back chasuble bottom,
⅛" in from the chasuble cut edge. Stitch in place ½"
from the chasuble edge. Press the bias strip to the
outside of the chasuble bottom along the seam
line to enclose the raw edges. Blind stitch in place.
Repeat along the front
edge (Figure 9-C18).

19. If you cut seven 30" by
2½" strips, piece them
following the general
instructions on page 48
to yield two 94" by 2½"
strips. With right sides
together, using a ¼"
seam, stitch one long
edge of the 94" by 2½"
strip of B to the same
of C. Press the seam
open. Press under ¼"
along the remaining
cut length of strip C.
Right sides together,
pin the remaining cut
length of B to the chas-
uble sleeve, extending
the ends at least ½"
beyond the finished
hem edges. Stitch strip
B to the chasuble using

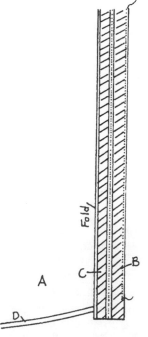

Figure 9-C19. Attaching
the sleeve binding.

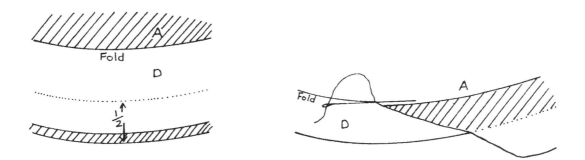

Figure 9-C18. The placement and stitching of the bias hem binding.

a ¼" seam, keeping strip C free (Figure 9-C19). Press the seam toward B.

20. With wrong sides together, press strip B-C in half exactly along the B-C seam line so that the folded edge of C meets and conceals the chasuble-B seam line. Pin, then blind stitch in place but leave 10" free at the four ends. Fold the ends of B-C inside out along the B-C seam line so that their right sides are together and their folded edges are aligned. Stitch along the bottom of each end, beginning even with the finished hem and stitching in an arc that follows the curve of the bottom hem (Figure 9-C20). Trim and turn right side out. Tuck the ends of the hem into the B-C strip. Pin the folded edge of C to the chasuble and blind stitch the C ends in place.

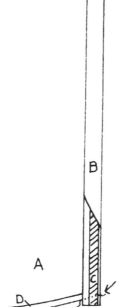

Figure 9-C20. Finishing the ends of the sleeve binding.

AN EVEN-WIDTH STOLE

Sizing

Adjust the length of the stole by lengthening or shorting the interfacing pattern piece.

Prepare the Yardage

1. Cut the following pieces:

Fabric	Quantity	Size
A	one	110½" x 2½"
B	one	110½" x 1¾"
C	one	110½" x 5¾"
D	two	2" x 2½"
		(optional for "kissing cross")
D	two	5¾" x 9"

Cut the Pattern

2. Draft the stole pattern by cutting a piece of non-fusible, midweight interfacing into a single strip measuring 116" by 4".

Making the Stole

3. Center the strip of fabric A along the length of the interfacing strip and baste in place. Strip A will be 2¾" short of both interfacing ends.

4. "Kissing cross" option: fold one of the 2" by 2½" D sections in half lengthwise, right sides together. Stitch both ends in a ¼" seam (Figure 9-S4a). Turn right side out, press, and label it Da. Press the remaining 2" by 2½" D section in half lengthwise, right side out. Mark the center neck line on the stole. Place the cut edges of the folded, unstitched section D ¼" beyond the center line; the ends will be flush with the cut edges of A. Pin and stitch through all thicknesses in a scant ½" seam (Figure 9-S4b). Trim the seam, press the folded edge of D over the seam, and blind stitch in place. Mark the center of the stole perpendicular to the crosswise center. Place the cut edges of section Da ¼" beyond the lengthwise center while extending the finished ends equally beyond the completed D section. Stitch in a scant ½" seam through all thickness (Figure 9-S4c). Trim. Press the folded edge over the seam and blind stitch the folded edge and finished ends in place to create a cross at the neck.

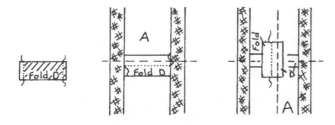

Figure 9-S4 a-c. The kissing cross.
a: Stitching the ends of one section D.
b: Placement of the other section D.
c: Placement of the section D from step 5a.

5. To continue with the stole: With right sides of stole together, align one long cut edge of B along one cut length of A. Stitch B to A through all thicknesses, using a ¼" seam. Press to relax the seam, then press seam and B away from A.

6. Right sides together, align one long cut edge of C along the remaining cut length of A. Stitch C to A through all thicknesses, using a ¼" seam. Press to relax the seam, then press the seam and C away from A.

7. Right sides together, align one 9" edge of D along the bottom edge of C-A-B, beginning flush with the outside edge of B (which extends ½" beyond the interfacing) and ending flush with the edge of C (Figure 9-S7). Stitch in a ¼" seam. Press D toward bottom of stole. Repeat for the other end.

8. Apply hem tape to both bottom cut edges of D, overlapping tape ¼".

9. With right sides together, fold the length of C-D back to the cut edge of B-D. Match the seam lines of D exactly. Pin. Stitch in a ½" seam the complete length of the stole. Press the seam to relax it. You now have a 4" inside-out tube.

10. Fold D up 3" to the outside of the tube (include width of hem tape in the 3"). The folded edge of D should be along the bottom edge of the interfacing. Blind stitch the hem in place, keeping the opposing sides of the tube free. Repeat on other end. Turn stole right side out and press.

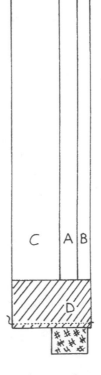

Figure 9-S7. Attaching D to C-A-B over interfacing.

AN EVEN-WIDTH MANIPLE

Prepare the Yardage

1. Cut the following pieces:

Fabric	Quantity	Size
A	one	34½" x 2½"
B	one	34½" x 6½"
D	two	3¾" x 8½"

Cut the Pattern

2. Draft the maniple pattern by cutting a piece of non-fusible, midweight interfacing into a single strip measuring 38" by 4".

Making the Maniple

3. Lay the strip of fabric A down the center of the interfacing strip and baste in place. Strip A will be 1¾" short of both interfacing ends.

4. With right sides together, align one long cut edge of B along one cut length of A. Stitch B to A through all thicknesses using a ¼" seam. Press to relax the seam, then press the seam and B away from A.

5. With right sides together, align one 8½" edge of D along the bottom edge of B-A beginning at the edge of A (¾" in from the interfacing edge) and extending the width of B-A (Figure 9-M5). Stitch in a ¼" seam. Press the seam and D toward the bottom of the maniple. Repeat for the other end.

6. Apply hem tape to both bottom cut edges of D, overlapping tape ¼".

7. With right sides together, fold the length of B-D back to the cut edge of A-D. Match the seam lines exactly. Pin. Stitch in a ¼" seam the complete length of B-D (Figure 9-M7). Press the seam.

8. With wrong sides together, fold B-D exactly along the

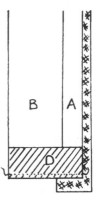

Figure 9-M5. Attaching D to B-A over interfacing.

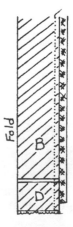

Figure 9-M7. Stitching B-D to A-D over interfacing.

long edge of the interfacing extension. Press. You now have an inside-out tube 4" wide with A centered between B and in perfect alignment with the interfacing.

9. Fold D up 2" to the outside of the tube (include width of hem tape in the 2"). The folded edge of D should be along the bottom edge of the interfacing. Blind stitch the hem in place, keeping opposing sides of the tube free. Repeat on other end. Turn maniple right side out by pulling it through one of the open hemmed ends. Attach elastic and tack sides following the general instructions on page 51.

THE DALMATIC

A simple chasuble-alb may be made from this pattern by:
■ using a white or neutral fabric;
■ omitting the orphreys and apparels, or using simple, neutral orphreys only;
■ lengthening the sleeves to reach the wrists, around 10";
■ lengthening the hem to reach the ankles, around 18";
■ stitching the sides closed from 8" below the dot to the hem, and using snaps to close the slit under the arms (from the dot to the point 8" below).

Cut the Pattern

1. Draft the dalmatic pattern following the general instructions on page 50.
2. Smooth out fabric A on a large flat surface, with the yardage folded in half lengthwise and the selvage edges together. Carefully fold the fabric over crosswise to quarter the fabric without wrinkles.
3. Lay the dalmatic pattern on the fabric with the sleeve top along the crosswise fold and the center front/back along the lengthwise fold (Figure 9-DT3). Cut it out along the bottom and side edges. Transfer the dot under the arm to all four thicknesses of the fabric. Remove the pattern.

Preparing the Fabric

4. Temporarily mark the fold along the sleeve top, then open out the crosswise fold of the fabric. Measure and draw a line the complete length of the fabric 5" in from the folded center (Figure 9-DT4).
5. Completely open out the fabric. Measure and draw a second line 10" parallel to the first line so that the two lines flank the center (see Figure 9-DT7).
6. Measure 9½" down from the shoulder fold on the

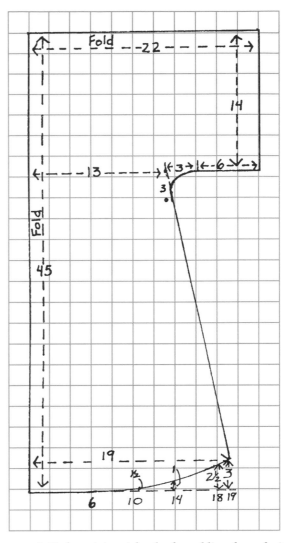

Pattern 9. Dalmatic/tunicle; draft neckline from facing. Scale: one square = 2 inches.

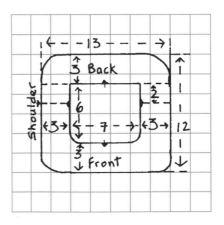

front and back (see Figure 9-DT7). Draw a horizontal line where marked.

7. Draw a second horizontal line, on the front and back, 18" down from and parallel to the first line

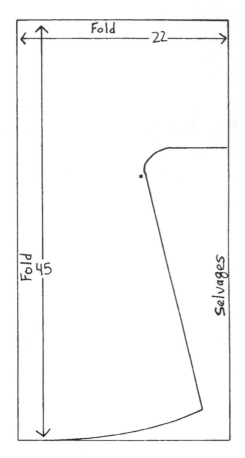

Figure 9-DT3. Dalmatic/tunicle pattern placement.

(Figure 9-DT7). Use your aesthetic judgment here. If you have altered the length of the dalmatic significantly, you may want to raise or lower this second line. Before applying the apparels and orphreys, make sure you have the center and shoulder lines clearly marked where they intersect.

8. From fabric B, cut four apparels measuring 8" by 10" and two orphreys measuring 8" by 90" (or your hem-to-hem length). Fold the apparels and orphreys in half lengthwise and press to a 4" folded width.

9. Pin and baste the four apparels to the dalmatic by aligning the apparel cut edges along the drawn horizontal lines between the two lengthwise lines. Be sure that all of the folded edges are toward the shoulder fold (Figure 9-DT9). Stitch in place ½" from the cut apparel edges. Press the four apparels toward the hemline. Blind stitch the folded edges in place.

10. Pin then baste the two orphreys to the dalmatic by aligning the orphrey cut edges along the drawn vertical lines. Have the folded edges face toward the center line (Figure 9-DT10). Stitch in place ½"

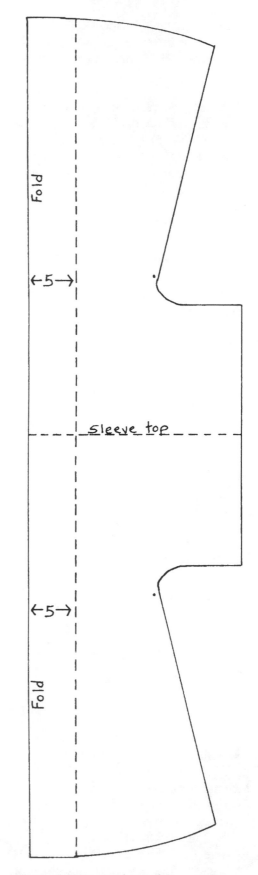

Figure 9-DT4. Orphrey placement line.

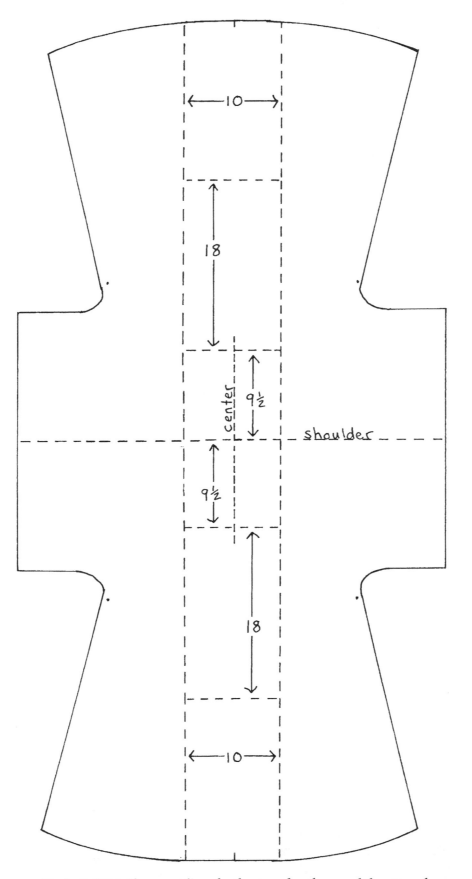

Figure 9-DT7. Placement lines for the second orphrey and the apparels.

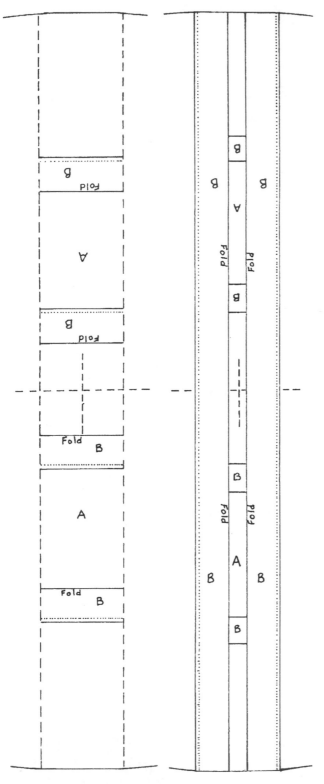

Figure 9-DT9.
Attaching the apparels.

Figure 9-DT10.
Attaching the orphreys.

from the cut orphrey edges. Press the two orphreys toward the dalmatic sides. Blind stitch the folded edges in place.

Finishing the Neckline

11. Draft the neck facing pattern 9 (page 99). Using the facing pattern, cut out the facing and the interfacing, making notches at the center front, back, and shoulder lines. Attach the interfacing to the facing following the general instructions on page 48. Finish the outside edge of the facing by turning it under ¼" and stitching or by serging.

12. Open out the dalmatic and smooth it on a large flat surface with the right side up. Right sides together, lay the neck facing on the dalmatic, matching the centers and the shoulder lines. Placing the facing will determine the dalmatic front and back. Be sure that the facing is exactly centered and straight between the orphreys (see Figure 9-C14, page 102). Pin and baste in place. Stitch ½" from the facing neck opening edge, pivoting at the corners. Finish in the same manner as the chasuble step 15 and Figure 9-C15 (page 102).

Finishing the Sleeves

13. Prepare the two 28" lengths of ¼" cording from fabric D as directed in the general instructions on page 49. Align the raw edges of the cording along the cut edge of the sleeve. Baste.

14. Cut two 4½" by 28" strips from fabric B and two 4½" by 28" from fabric C for the sleeve orphreys and facing. Right sides together, stitch the length of a strip B to a C in a ½" seam. Repeat with the remaining two strips. Press each strip B-C in half lengthwise along the seam. Press under ½" along each remaining cut length of C.

15. With right sides together, pin the long cut edge of B to the sleeve edge. Baste. Using a zipper foot, stitch a ½" seam through all thicknesses. Press B away from the sleeve. Repeat with the other sleeve.

Finishing the Sides

16. Cut four side facings measuring 4" by 26" (or the length from the underarm dot to the hem) from the facing fabric and from the lightweight interfacing. Trim and attach the interfacing following the general instructions on page 48. Finish the top and one long edge of each facing, making sure you have two fronts and two backs (Figure 9-DT16).

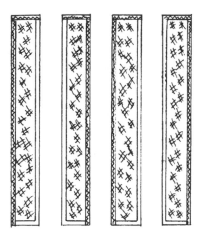

Figure 9-DT16. Two back and two front side facings.

17. With right sides together, pin one facing to the dalmatic side edge, extending the finished top edge of the facing ½" above the underarm dot and having the raw edges even. Stitch in a ½" seam from the dot to the hem. Press the facing open and understitch. Repeat for the other three facings and side edges (see Figure 9-DT18).

18. Keeping the side facings free and with the right sides together, pin side seams from the underarm dot to the end of the sleeve facings C (Figure 9-DT18). At the meeting of the cording, push one cord toward the sleeve and the other toward the dalmatic so that the seams meet, but the cording bulk is deferred to either side. Stitch the side seam in a ½" seam. To finish the seam, either serge or zigzag close to the first stitching. If zigzagged, trim excess seam allowance.

19. Turn the sleeve facing C under along the B-C seam line so that the folded edge of C meets the stitching line of the sleeve to B. Blind stitch the folded edge in place to conceal the seam.

Finishing the Hem

20. Open out the side facings and measure up a 2" hem. Ease stitch, then finish the cut hem edge with lace tape, serging, or turning under ¼". Tuck the end of the facing in a 45 degree angle within the 2" hem allowance (see Figure 9-DT18). If the wearer is available to try on the dalmatic, check for an even hang of the hem. Adjust if necessary. Blind stitch hem in place, pulling up ease stitching where necessary along the curved edge to smooth out the hem.

21. Fold the side facing to the inside, easing the length to conform to the hem curve. Pin. Whip stitch the

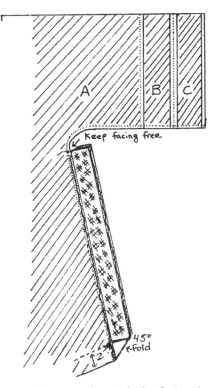

Figure 9-DT18. Understitch the facing (step 17), the underarm seam (step 18), and the 45 degree hem fold (step 20).

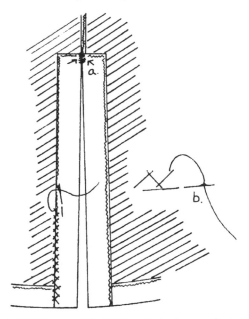

Figure 9-DT21 a and b. Whip stitch the top facing extensions and catch stitch the sides working from left to right. Make a small horizontal stitch in the facing about a ¼" from the finished edge. Then, diagonally across from the first stitch near the facing edge, make another small horizontal stitch in fabric A. Alternate stitches along the edge in a zigzag fashion.

½" extension above the underarm dot to support the side seam (Figure 9-DT21a). Catch stitch the side facings in place (Figure 9-DT21b). Blind stitch the hemline closed.

THE TUNICLE

Make the tunicle in the same manner as the dalmatic except: cut the sleeve and hem length 2" shorter; cut two apparels 7" by 10"; cut the orphreys 7" by 86"; omit step 7 since there is no lower set of apparels; and cut the sleeve orphreys and facings 4" wide.

A WESTERN DEACON'S STOLE

Sizing

If the bottom section of the stole needs lengthening or shortening, see the general instructions on pages 51–52.

Prepare the Yardage

1. Cut the following:

Fabric	Section	Quantity	Size
A	g	one	2½" x 48"
A	h	two	2½" x 16½"
B	g	one	1¾" x 49"
B	h	two	1¾" x 17"
B	i	two	5" x 9½"
C	g	one	1¾" x 46"
C	h	two	1¾" x 16"
C	i	two	5" x 1½"
C	j	one	5" x 49"
C	k	two	5" x 28"
D		two	5" x 2½"

Cut the Pattern

2. Draft the deacon's stole pattern (page 50) onto midweight interfacing. Trim away ¾" from both sides of the width of both sections so that the width measures 4".

Making the Deacon's Stole

3. Lay the strip of fabric Ag down the center of the interfacing strip for section 1 and baste in place. Do the same with strip Ah on both interfacing section 2 pieces by placing Ah 11" short of the interfacing ends toward the bottom.

4. With right sides together, align one long edge of Bg along one length of Ag, and align each Bh

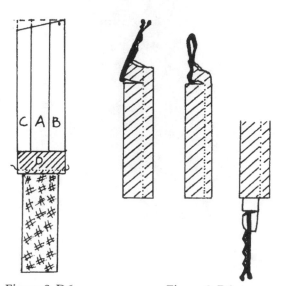

Figure 9-D6.
Attaching D to a section 2 C-A-B strip over interfacing.

Figure 9-D8.
Turning a narrow tube with a bobby pin.

along Ah. Using a ¼" seam, stitch Bg to Ag and Bh to Ah through all thicknesses. Press seams, Bg and Bh to the outside, extending them ½" beyond the interfacing.

5. Stitch Cg to the remaining cut length of Ag, and Ch to Ah. Trim the ends of section 1 to match the angle of the interfacing, then trim what you can from the interfacing to make it ½" short of the angled fabric. Do the same for the angled tops of section 2. Retain the dots marked on the interfacing.

6. Right sides together, align one 5" edge of D along the bottom edge of one section 2 C-A-B strip (Figure 9-D6). Stitch in a ¼" seam. Press D toward the bottom of the stole. Repeat for the other section 2 end.

7. Add piece Ci to D in the same manner, and then attach Bi, trimming interfacing ½" shorter than Bi.

8. Cut a 1½" by 3½" piece from fabric B. Fold the piece in half lengthwise, right sides together. Stitch into a narrow tube using a ¼" seam. Snip ½" across one folded end. Slip a bobby pin onto the snipped fold, then turn the bobby pin into the tube and push it through until the tube is turned right side out (Figure 9-D8). Press and trim off the snipped fold to achieve a 3" by ½" tube. Use this in place of the ribbon to secure the deacon's stole under the arm.

9. Complete the stole following the general instructions for the deacon's stole on page 52, using pieces Cj and Ck for the lining. Make sure you line up the C-A-B seams exactly.

A TABBED BURSE

Prepare the Yardage

1. Cut the following:

Fabric	Quantity	Size
A	two	10" squares
B	two	10" squares
B	one	7" x 10"
B	one	1½" x 6½"
Batiste	two	10" squares

2. Draw a line along the lengthwise grain 4" in from one cut edge of one A square (see Figure 9-B3a).

3. Fold the 7" by 10" strip B in half, wrong sides together, to create a folded piece 3½" by 10". Align the cut edges of strip B to the drawn line on A, with the folded edge of B toward the 4" side of A. Pin and stitch in place using a ½" seam (Figure 9-B3a). Press the folded edge of B over the seam toward the center of A (Figure 9-B3b). Blind stitch the folded edge of B in place.

4. Baste the batiste to the wrong side of both fabric A squares.

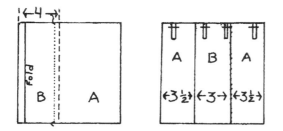

Figure 9-B3 a and b. Placement of burse orphrey.

Making the Burse

5. Cut a 1½" by 6½" strip from B, then fold it in half lengthwise, right sides together. Stitch the long cut edge in a ¼" seam. Turn the tube in the same manner described in Figure 9-D8 (page 110). Cut the turned tube into four 1½" pieces. Across the back edge and on the right side of the appareled burse top, space the four pieces evenly, with the raw edges even. Begin and end 1" from the outside edges (see Figure 9-B3b). Baste in place.

6. With right sides together, pin one B square (lining) to the burse cover, leaving a side edge open. Stitch the back edge with the four tube strips, an adjoining side, and the front edge closed in a ½" seam. Trim seam and notch corners. Turn right side out and press.

7. Lay the remaining A square right side up. Overlay the burse top right sides together, with the raw edges of the tabs along the back cut edge. Baste the tabs in place (Figure 9-B7).

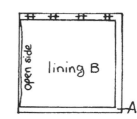

Figure 9-B7. Placement of the tabs and turned burse top on the burse bottom.

8. Right sides together, lay the remaining B lining square over all and pin along three sides: the back with the basted tabs, the side with the burse top opening, and the front. Fold the burse top inside to avoid catching it when stitching the burse bottom sections together. Stitch the three pinned sides closed with a ½" seam. Trim seam and notch corners. Turn right side out, pulling out the burse top. Press.

9. Press the burse top and bottom open sides in ½" (Figure 9-B9). Close the burse to make sure that the top and bottom edges line up exactly. Insert the two Plexiglas™ sheets into the burse side openings. Slip stitch the side openings closed.

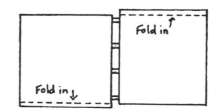

Figure 9-B9. Closing the burse sides.

A CORDED CHALICE VEIL

Prepare the Yardage

1. Cut the following pieces:

Fabric	Quantity	Size
A	two	11" x 25"
B	one	4" x 25"
B	one	8" x 25"
C	one	25" square
D	one	18" square for cording bias strips

2. Rights sides together and using ¼" seams, join the two A strips to the opposing long edges of the 4" by 25" B strip. Press the seams toward B. You now have a single piece A-B-A that measures 25" square.

3. Draw a line perpendicular to the B strip, 11¼"
   from one A-B-A edge (Figure 9-V3). Fold the 8"
   by 25" B strip in half to yield a folded strip that
   measures 4" by 25". Align the cut edges of the
   folded strip to the drawn line, with the folded
   edge toward the 11¼" width. Pin and stitch in a
   ½" seam.

4. Press the folded edge of B toward the center of A-
   B-A and blind stitch the folded edge in place to
   create a cross (see the illustration at the beginning
   of this chapter).

Making the Chalice Veil

5. Make a narrow cording following the general
   instructions (page 49) and attach it to the outside
   perimeter of the chalice veil top.

6. Finish the chalice veil according to the general
   instructions on page 53. Use the square cut from
   fabric C for the lining.

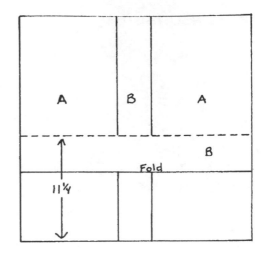

Figure 9-V3.
Placement of the chalice veil cross orphrey.

NOTES

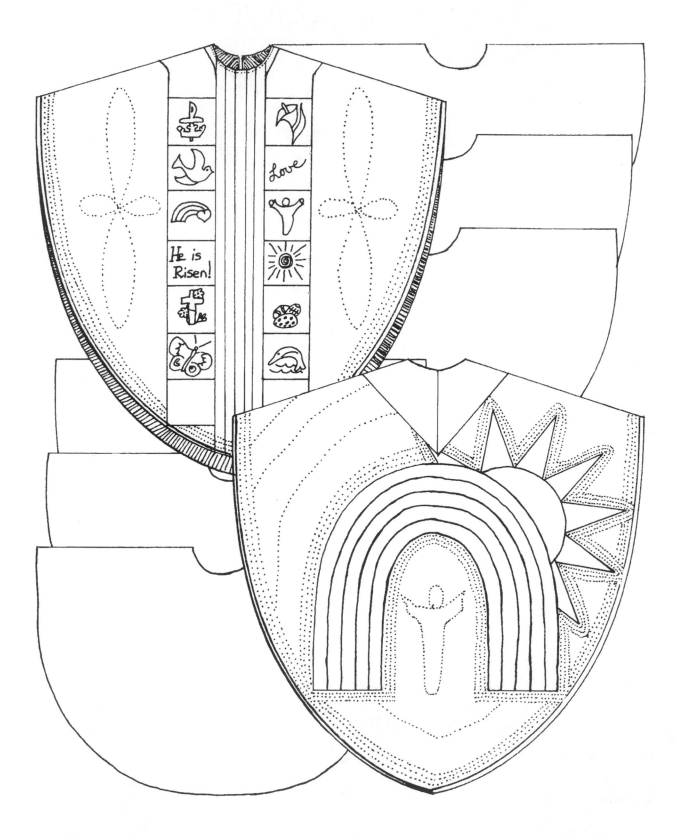

He is Risen!

Love

10.
A Child's Easter

⁓

This is the day that the LORD has made; let us rejoice and be glad in it.

—Psalm 118:24

The central season of the church year, Easter marks the resurrection of Jesus Christ, who conquered death and won immortality for humanity. Easter joy, Easter peace, and Easter victory are the message during this fifty-day season. Selected readings are full of references to the risen Jesus, and worshipers are invited to realize, ever more deeply and personally, that Jesus triumphed over death and is present to us. The final word is victory and new life, not evil, suffering, and death.

The Easter chasuble and stole patterns described in this chapter are simple, youthful, and happy. A variation of the stiff Latin style, the chasuble is designed to complement an overlay stole displaying squares created by children. The chasuble features tapered sleeves with a close-fitting neckline, slashed in the back. It is made from plain white cotton with satin machine appliqué and quilting. The rainbow with the sun rising behind it reminds us that God has kept a promise to never again curse the ground (Genesis 9) and that God has redeemed humanity through the rising of the Son. Because the other church seasons emanate from Easter, all liturgical colors are used to make the rainbow. Rose or pink, as a reminder that the resurrection occurred at dawn, is a suitable color for the lining.

Sky blue cotton is the base color for the overlay stole, while the children's assortment of colors and designs make for a celebratory and welcoming final product. If the number of children (or intergenerational participants) exceeds the twelve squares called for in the pattern, use the excess squares for a deacon's stole, frontal, and/or pulpit hangers. Refer to the general instructions for guidelines on making the paraments (page 53).

Finally, a pattern for a child-size chasuble is included. The child's chasuble is an excellent teaching tool, especially if you make one in each of the liturgical colors. They may be used solely for classroom instruction, or the child who leads the others into church at the Offertory may wear it as a sign of the children's integral participation in the Great Thanksgiving. Use an interesting fabric to make up the chasubles, or have the children create adornments appropriate to each season.

FABRIC REQUIREMENTS

Chasuble (44" wide, 44" long in front and 46" long in back, finished)

Chasuble fabric, a good-bodied white cotton: 2⅔ yards of at least a 44" width.

Lining fabric, a good-bodied rose cotton: 2⅔ yards of at least a 44" width.

Appliqué fabric, five compatible satins at least 44" wide, preferably: ½ yard each of rose and green; ⅝ yard of blue; ⅔ yard of purple; and ¾ yard of red.

Sun appliqué fabric, a bright, clear yellow satin: ⅓ yard.

Lightweight batting: 2⅔ yards of 44" width or 1⅓ yards of 90" width. Choose a batting that does not require quilting closer than every 6". Warm & Natural,™ Morning Glory,™ Hobbs Thermore,™ or Quilter's Dream™ are good choices.

Sulky Totally Stable™ or other appliqué stabilizer: 1⅓ yards of 20" width.

White or yellow packaged double-fold quilt binding: 6 yards, or an extra ⅔ yard of the white cotton, or ⅔ yard total of the yellow satin.

Tear-away stabilizer: 2 yards.

Basting adhesive: optional.

Stole (5" wide by 110" long, finished)

Sky blue cotton: 1½ yards of 44" width (the color should complement the rainbow satins).

Bleached muslin, optional: ⅓ yard of 44" width.

Non-fusible, light to midweight interfacing: 1½ yards.

Fabric art supplies such as fabric paint and crayons, photo transfer paper, computer printer fabric, paper-backed iron-on adhesive, embroidery floss, manufactured appliqués, lace and ribbons.

Gold chain or cording to hold back neckline in place: 6"–8" length, optional.

Child's chasuble (39" wide by 35" long in front and in back, finished)

2 yards; if lined, another 2 yards for lining.

A STIFFENED CHASUBLE

Sizing

These directions are for a small, batted chasuble. Make size adjustments at the time of pattern drafting.

Draft the Pattern

1. Draft chasuble pattern 10 on page 119 by following the general instructions on page 50.
2. Cut the appliqué stabilizer in half to make two 24" by 20" sections. Butt the two sections together along one 24" edge and tack together by hand, using a wide zigzag stitch to yield a 24" by 40" piece of stabilizer. Draft the rainbow, sun, and seven rays directly onto the non-adhesive side of the stabilizer. Each rainbow arc is 1½" wide; the completed rainbow measures 24" high by 26" wide. (Pattern is on page 123)

Prepare the Yardage

1. Cut the chasuble, chasuble lining, and batting from the drafted pattern, being sure that the centers are along the lengthwise fold of the fabric. Transfer the dot for the point of the back neck slash. On the chasuble pieces, lightly mark the center front line from neck to hem. Lightly press

in a crease along the center back line. Mark the cutting line from the neck edge to the dot on the center back.

2. From each of the five satins used in the rainbow, cut one strip 1½" by 43" (adjust length if you altered the pattern length).
3. Carefully cut out the rainbow and sun pieces from the stabilizer. Following the manufacturer's directions, press the inside rainbow curve onto the right side of the rose satin. Cut the rose satin exactly along the inside curve and bottom edge of the stabilizer. When cutting along the outside curve, add a ¼" seam allowance (see Figure 10-C4). Do the same with the remaining rainbow pieces in the following color order: rose, green, blue, purple, red. Do not add the ¼" seam allowance to the outside curve of the final red piece. Apply the sun and the seven ray stabilizer pieces to the right side of the yellow satin. When you cut out the satin, add a ¼" seam allowance along the bottom edge of the sun and at the base of the rays.
4. With right side up, smooth the chasuble back on a large flat surface. Center the smallest rainbow arc, rose, on the chasuble back, with its inside center point 12" below the bottom point of the neckline slash. To assure that the rainbow sits straight on the chasuble, align the lower 5" of the inside

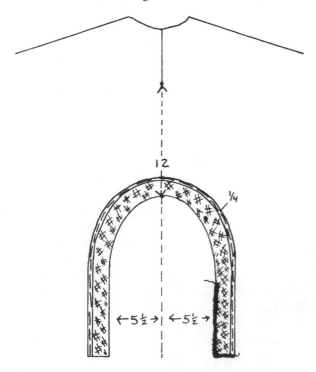

Figure 10-C4. Placement of the inside arc of the rainbow on the chasuble back.

arc legs 5½" parallel to the center fold (Figure 10-C4). Pin the arc and baste the seam allowance in place. Machine appliqué with a satin stitch along the bottom and inside edges. Add the next arc in the same manner, being sure to overlap the inside edge of the adjacent arc over the seam allowance of the previous arc—the stabilizer edges will butt together exactly. Do not stitch the final outside edge of the rainbow, the red arc, until after the sun has been applied.

5. Smooth the chasuble back on a large flat surface. Insert the seam allowance of the sun base under the top rainbow arc. Place the sun to either side of the apex at a pleasing position (see the illustration at the beginning of this chapter). Insert the seam allowances of the rays under the sun, butting the base of each ray to its neighbor until all are positioned around the sun. Trim the two end rays so they fit smoothly under the top arc. Look at the chasuble back and adjust the sun placement if necessary to please the eye. Pin and baste all of the pieces in position. Machine appliqué the rays, then the sun. Finish with the outside edge of the top rainbow arc. Remove the stabilizer(s).

6. Smooth out the chasuble back on a large smooth surface. With a fine marking pencil, such as Roxanne's silver or a 3H graphite, lightly mark some simple quilting lines beyond the echo quilting (see step 13). The chasuble need not be heavily quilted but should have enough quilting to stabilize the batting. The chapter divider drawing shows some suggested quilting. The arcs to the left are spaced 4" apart. Set the back of the chasuble aside.

7. Lay the chasuble front on a smooth flat surface. Right side up, center the middle color (blue) of the 1½" by 42" strips along the center front line. Baste in place. Right sides together, align one edge of the green strip along the left edge of the middle strip. Pin and stitch using a ¼" seam. Press this strip open. Add the purple strip in the same manner along the right edge of the middle strip. Press under ¼" along one long edge of the two remaining strips (rose and red). Add the rose strip to the green raw edge and the red strip to the purple free edge in the same manner described above. Blind stitch the folded edge of the end strips in place (Figure 10-C7).

Or, stabilize the strips with 1" widths of an adhesive stabilizer. Cut the middle strip with a ¼" seam allowance on each side to yield a 1½" wide strip; add a ¼" seam allowance on the outside edge of the second and fourth strips to yield 1¼"

Machine Appliqué Tips

- Use silk pins that are thin with sharp points to avoid unsightly holes and distortion.
- Use a size 8 needle that is thin, enters the fabric easily, and won't leave large holes. If you use rayon thread, use a size 11 or 12 machine embroidery needle.
- A walking foot is invaluable for keeping the appliqué stable; an appliqué foot is a less expensive and suitable alternative.
- A basting adhesive may be used to hold the appliqué in place while stitching.
- The top thread should be a cotton or rayon embroidery thread. Match each fabric closely. The bobbin thread may be a neutral color of cotton embroidery thread or a pre-wound cotton bobbin made for machine embroidery.
- Loosen your upper machine tension 1–2 digits so that the bobbin thread does not show on top; instead, the top thread will be pulled to the underside.

- Practice stitching on a scrap of satin on cotton. To satin stitch, use a medium to medium-narrow zigzag stitch and adjust the length until the stitches are side by side without gaps or overlapping. The stitch width should extend just beyond the outside edge of the appliqué.
- You will achieve the best results if you use a tear-away stabilizer or freezer paper underneath the chasuble fabric for added support.
- As you stitch around the curve of the arc, stop and pivot regularly to maintain a smooth stitch. At the sun ray points, gradually reduce the stitch width, stop, pivot, and then gradually increase to the initial stitch width.
- Stitch through all thicknesses, including the stabilizer. Carefully remove the stabilizer after the stitching is complete. Use tweezers to remove small pieces that get stuck in the stitching.

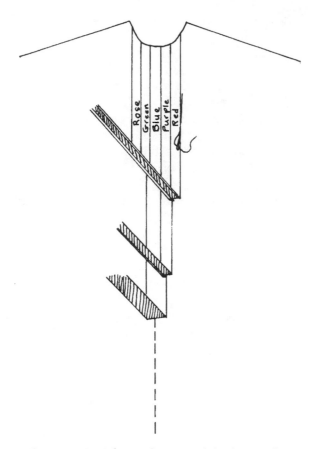

Figure 10-C7. The application of the front pillar.

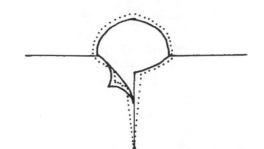

Figure 10-C10. Stay stitch the neck edge and slash.

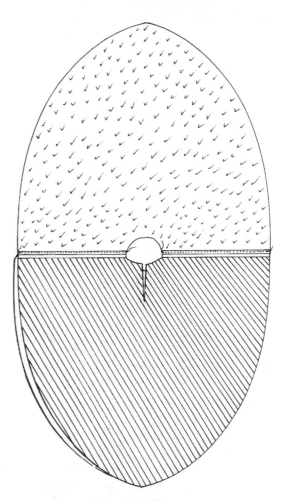

Figure 10-C11.
Attach the batting to the shoulder seam allowances.

wide strips, and cut the end strips 1" wide. Machine appliqué in the same manner as the rainbow, only begin with the middle strip, overlapping as you work outward.

Once the strips are appliquéd in place, trim the bottom edge to match the hem curve and the top edge to match the neckline. Remove the stabilizer, if used.

8. In the same manner as in step 6, lightly mark quilting lines on the chasuble front. Remember the overlay stole will cover up to 5" on either side of the central pillar.

Stitching the Chasuble

9. Right sides together, align the chasuble shoulder edges. Pin and stitch the shoulder seams in a ½" seam. Press the seam open. Stitch the shoulder seams of the lining.

10. Stay stitch the neck edge and both sides of the slash opening on the chasuble and the lining, tapering the stitching close to the cutting line as you reach the point and pivoting at the point (Figure 10-C10). Cut the slash open, being careful not to cut through the stitching.

11. Trim the ½" seam allowance away from the shoulder and neck edges of the batting. On a large flat surface, smooth the lining wrong side up. Insert the batting under the folded-over seam allowance along the shoulders. Baste the batting to the seam

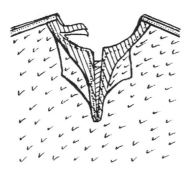

Figure 10-C12.
Stitch the neck edge and slash,
keeping the batting free.

allowance, being careful not to catch the lining. Understitch the batting to the shoulder seam allowances, keeping the lining free (Figure 10-C11). Hand baste the batting to the lining along the neck edge and outside edges.

12. With right sides together, pin and baste the chasuble to the lining along the neck edge and back slash opening—do not catch it in the batting. Stitch in a ½" seam around the neck edge, pivot at the corners, and taper to a narrow seam as you stitch the slash (Figure 10-C12). Within 2" of the slash point, change to a smaller stitch length and take one or two small stitches across the point. Clip the slash opening to the machine stitching, being careful not to cut through the stitching. Trim, grade, and clip the neck seam. Turn the lining and batting to the inside of the chasuble. Use a point turner to carefully push out the corners. Press. Topstitch the neck edge and slash opening ½" in from the seam, being sure to catch the batting.

13. Smooth the lining, batting, and chasuble on a large flat surface. Hand baste the layers together in 6" parallel rows across the width of the chasuble. Machine quilt the layers with a walking foot and machine quilting needle, or quilt by hand. Quilt in the ditch (seam) between each satin color on the front pillar, along one edge of the satin stitch of each rainbow color, and where the rays meet with the sun. Use thread to match each color or use clear nylon .004 quilting thread. Echo quilt three rows of white stitching spaced ½" apart

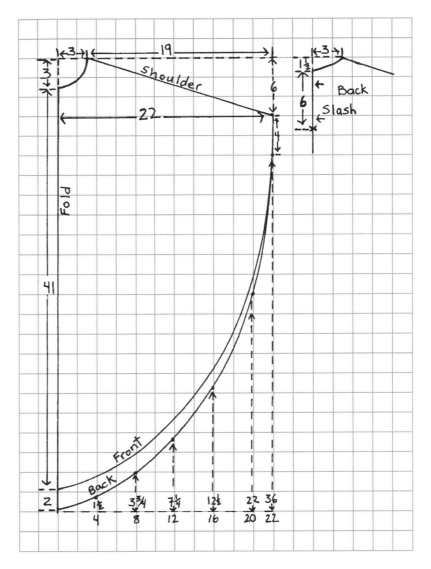

Pattern 10. Chasuble. Cut one front and one back on fold.
Scale: one square = 2 inches.

completely around the rainbow, sun, front pillar, and on the marked quilting lines (see chapter divider drawing).

14. Beginning 2" in from the outside edge, quilt the perimeter of the chasuble, skipping over other quilting that may extend close to the outside edge. (To begin and end machine quilting, set the stitch length at 0 and take a few stitches to lock the threads.) Repeat with two more rows of quilting spaced ½" apart toward the outside edge. (See chapter divider drawing.) Trim the outside edge, if necessary, for a clean, even perimeter. Trim the chasuble top a scant ¼" inside the batting and lining edges. Remove the basting.

Finishing the Hemline

15. Use packaged quilt binding or follow the general instructions on page 48. Cut and join 6 yards of 2½" wide bias strips of the chasuble white fabric or yellow satin for the chasuble binding (adjust length if you altered the overall size of the chasuble). Press the binding in half lengthwise to make a strip 1¼" wide. Apply the binding to finish the chasuble edge in the manner described in the general instructions, page 48.

A PATCHWORK OVERLAY STOLE

Sizing

Adjust the length of the stole by lengthening or shortening the pattern. The stole should hang a few inches short of the finished chasuble.

Cut the Pattern

1. Draft the stole pattern 10 on page 122 following the instructions on page 50. Cut its full length from the lining and the interfacing. Cut the stole top at the cut-off line on the pattern (Figure 10-S1). If you are using more or fewer squares than called for, you may need to adjust this cutting line. If in doubt, cut long. You can always trim it off later.

Prepare the Yardage

2. If you are using the blue for the square base, cut fourteen 6" squares. Or, if you are using bleached muslin squares, cut the following pieces:

Fabric	Quantity	Size
Muslin	twelve	5" squares
Blue	two	6" squares
Blue	twenty-four	1¼" x 4½" strips
Blue	twenty-four	1¼" x 6" strips

3. On the muslin squares or all except two of the blue squares, draw a ½" seam allowance just inside all four edges and ask the children to keep their work inside the marked lines.

4. Have the children design and complete symbols in each square. Read the Easter story and allow the children to come up with their own symbols and designs in response to the story. Some traditional Easter symbols include: the butterfly, egg, lily, lamb, empty or flowered cross, rainbow, and

sunrise. Children should not be limited to these suggestions; they should be encouraged to design their own symbols. If children resist making a symbol, suggest that they use manufactured appliqués. It's easy to make them by applying paper-backed fusible web to a fabric motif. You can use the children's own art, utilizing fabric paint, markers or crayons, embroidery, photo transfer paper, or computer scans of their drawings. Basic directions for using these items are supplied below. Many wonderful products are available for decorating fabric squares. Check with you local craft store for ideas and instructions.

Making the Stole

Figure 10-S1.
Cut two of the
stole top.

Figure 10-S5.
A muslin square
bordered in stole fabric.

5. If you used blue squares, skip to step 6. For muslin, once all of the squares are imaged, trim them to 4½" square. On two opposing sides of each square, right sides together, pin a 1¼" by 4½" strip. Stitch in a ¼" seam and press open. On the remaining two sides, pin and stitch a 1¼" by 6" strip. Press open to yield a framed 6" square (Figure 10-S5; see also Figures 7-B2 and B3, page 80).

6. Lay out the completed squares in two rows. Move them around until you are satisfied with their arrangement. Alternate heavy and light images, and try to have directional images facing inward. Once arranged, pin the bottom of the top square of each row to the top of the next square. Stitch in a ½" seam. Press open. Continue adding squares to each row until all of the squares are used. Watch to make sure they line up straight. After the bottom-imaged square is stitched in place, add a plain 6" square to the bottom of each row.

7. Pin and stitch in a ½" seam the top of each row to the bottom of each stole top cut out in step 1. Be sure to have the correct row on the left and right sides of the stole and check the overall length. Trim the bottom edge of the stole tops, if necessary, to keep the stole short of the chasuble.

8. Apply the interfacing to the stole lining following the general instructions on page 48.

9. Stitch the center back seam of the stole and lining, stopping and backstitching ½" short of the inner neck edge (this will allow you to turn the inside V smoothly). Apply a kissing cross if desired— or apply a design made by the children to the stole back.

10. Finish the stole following the general instructions on page 51. If desired, tack a chain or cording at the dots on the neckline (4" up from the center back seam) to hold the stole in place.

Decorating Fabric Squares

- Permanent fabric markers and paint are readily available at craft stores; apply them directly to the fabric as if it were paper (see chapter 11).

- Fabric crayons require that you trace the mirror image of the drawing onto a second piece of paper. Have the child color in the traced design with the fabric crayons. Transfer the mirrored coloring in the same manner as described below for photo transfer paper. The colors will be muted; a poly-cotton blend works best.

- Paper-backed fusible web is a simple way to apply an existing motif found on a fabric. Check the manufacturer's directions to confirm these basic instructions. Preheat iron to medium-high (dry silk, no steam). Place the fabric to be cut out and fused wrong side up on the ironing board and iron. Cut a piece of paper-backed fusible web slightly larger than the motif (but smaller than the fabric swatch), and place it paper side up over the motif. Glide the iron across the paper for one to two seconds. Do not over-iron; more heat is not better. Allow the web to cool before cutting out the motif. Remove the paper backing and place the motif, right side up, on the fabric square. Cover with a protective cloth or paper. Iron for ten to thirty seconds to fuse. Remove press cloth and cool before checking the bond. If a light web is used, machine or hand appliqué the outside edges; if a heavy web is used, seal the edges with a clear or colored fabric paint—do not stitch through heavy web on the machine.

- Photo transfer paper is a great way to apply photos or drawings to fabric. The colors will transfer best onto tightly woven muslin. Take the colored design or photo and photo transfer paper to a copy shop and have them photocopy the image onto your transfer paper with a *mirror* image using a good color copier. Preheat an iron to high (dry cotton setting, no steam) for five minutes. Cut off the excess transfer paper from the image. Place the muslin square right side up on the ironing board. Just before transferring the image, iron the fabric to preheat it. Place the image, transfer side down, on the heated fabric and iron it for twenty-five to thirty seconds to transfer the image onto the fabric. The key is to use even, firm pressure while moving the iron around to avoid scorching. While it's still hot, peel off the paper. Begin at one corner and peel slowly. If the transfer is still on the paper, stop peeling, replace the paper, and iron ten to twenty seconds more until the paper removes cleanly. Turn the fabric over and press it to set the image. Do not iron the transfer directly—it may stick to your iron. To iron it from the top side, cover it with a press cloth.
Note: You may decide to have the copy store transfer the colored symbols directly onto the fabric for you with their two-stage color transfer process. This eliminates the transfer paper but may be a bit pricey. The method described above is simple and satisfying.

- Computer scanning is another way to transfer an image directly onto fabric. It requires a color printer and computer printer fabric. Scan colored symbols into the computer; with the image on screen, test print on paper. When you are satisfied with the print, print onto computer printer fabric, trim to a 4½" square, and remove the paper backing.

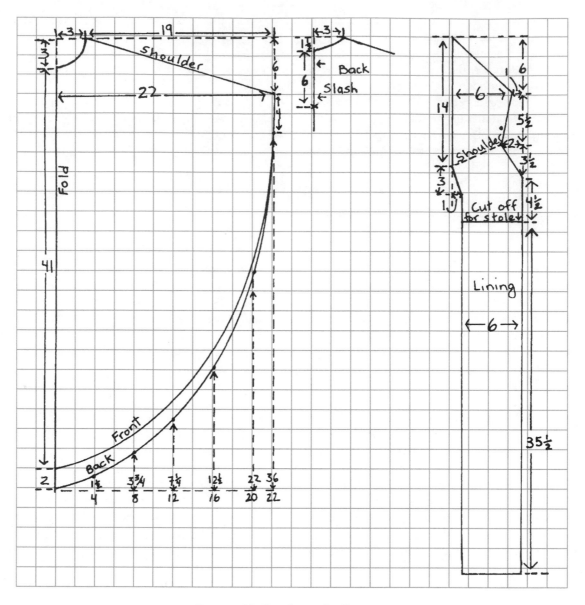

Pattern 10. Overlay stole. Cut two.
Scale: one square = 2 inches.

THE CHILD'S CHASUBLE

Sizing

The child's chasuble fits the average seven- to twelve-year-old. The neckline is the same in front and back so that even young children can put it on it correctly. If the width and length need to be adjusted, alter the outside measurements when you draft the pattern. To alter the neck opening, see the instructions for chasuble in chapter 6, step 1 (page 60).

Making the Chasuble

1. Draft the child's chasuble (Pattern 10) following the general instructions on page 50.
2. Cut out the chasuble and lining, if applicable, being sure to place the center front and back along the lengthwise fold and the shoulder lines along the crosswise fold—see Figures 7-C4 and 5 (page 75). Since the child's chasuble is the same, front and back, you may cut both sides simultaneously

by quartering the fabric: fold it at the shoulder line and cut. By making just three chasubles, you can have all six liturgical colors if you line them in different colors and reverse them.

3. Complete all ornamentation, back and front, if desired. An interesting fabric is often sufficient— or the children may want to put their own designs on solid colors using any of the methods in this book. Stay stitch the chasuble and lining neck edges.

If lined:

4. With right sides together, smooth fabric over lining, matching outer edges and neckline exactly. Pin outer edge all the way around front and back. Baste, then stitch in a ½" seam.

5. Clip curves. Turn right sides out pulling through the neck. Press edges flat.

6. Finish the neck edge by turning the fabric and lining under ½" all around, clipping where necessary within the stay-stitching to make a smooth fold. The folded edges of the fabric and lining should meet neatly. Baste, then blind stitch closed.

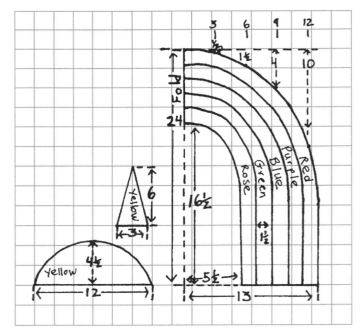

Pattern 10. Sun, ray, and rainbow adornments.
Scale: one square = 2 inches.

7. Topstitch or apply a decorative braid around neck and outside edges, if desired.

If unlined:

8. Bind the neck edge following the general instructions for binding found on page 48. Use a commercial binding if a color match is available.

9. Narrow hem the outside perimeter by hand or machine. Measure a ⅝" hem and ease stitch ¼" from raw edge around the curves. Turn the chasuble edge in ¼" and press. Turn the edge again ⅜" and press along the hemline, easing where necessary to maintain the grain alignment and a smooth hem. Topstitch by machine or blind stitch by hand.

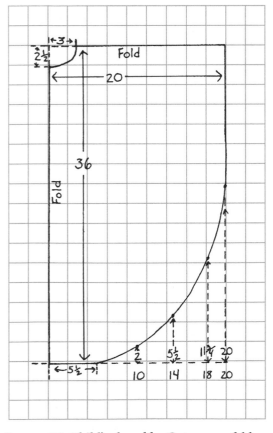

Pattern 10. Child's chasuble. Cut one on folds.
Scale: one square = 2 inches.

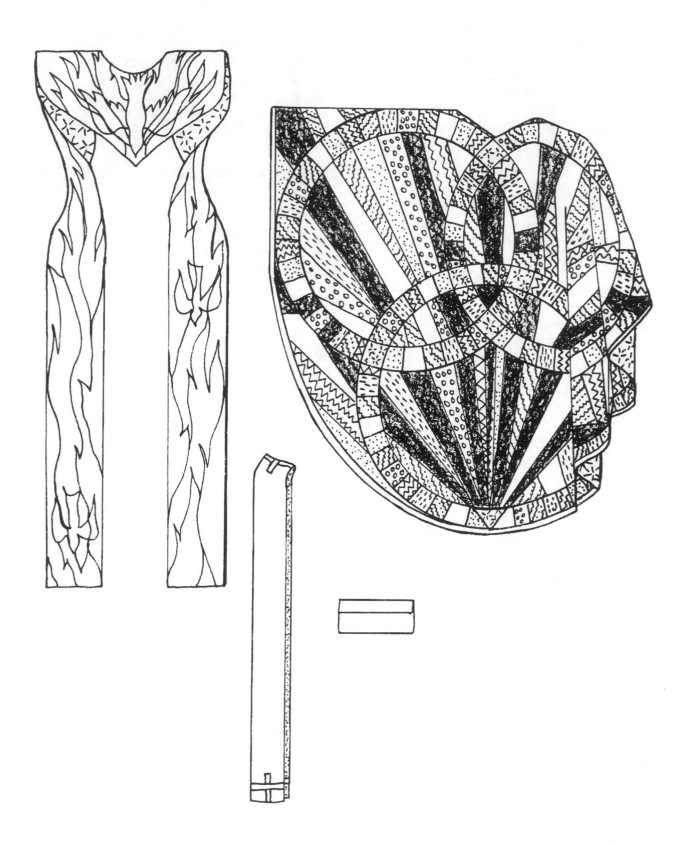

11.
COOL COTTON FOR A FIERY PENTECOST

∽

God's love has been poured into our hearts through the Holy Spirit that has been given to us.

—Romans 5:5

On the fiftieth day after Easter, the church celebrates Pentecost, the coming of the Holy Spirit. Empowered by their encounter with the Holy Spirit, the disciples bear courageous witness that Jesus is the risen Lord, fulfilling the prophecies and hopes of Israel. Witnesses are sent out to the whole world to love, share, and serve the Lord. The coming of the Holy Spirit marks the continuous presence of the risen Lord, enables all the baptized to minister in Jesus' name, and brings grace to all.

The season of Pentecost is the longest in the church, extending from mid-spring to late fall, when the First Sunday of Advent recommences the church year. For nearly half a year, the Pentecost season, commonly called "ordinary time," concentrates on Jesus' public ministry of proclamation, signs, healing, and teaching. Christians are invited to consider Jesus' message on a regular basis in hopes that they may grow in grace in their daily lives. The church year ends with the Feast of Christ the King; he is the one who brings all things together under a cosmic and most gracious rule. Through Christ all are gifted by the Creator and, in turn, all are gifted back to the Creator.

While the season of Pentecost champions green, symbolic of hope, growth, and eternity, the color for Pentecost Sunday is red, the color of the Holy Spirit and the flames of fire that descended on the disciples in Jerusalem (Acts 2:1–4). Red is rarely worn except on Pentecost Sunday, during Holy Week, on the feasts of martyrs, and for ordinations. A stole worn over an alb or chasuble-alb is often indicated, making a red overlay stole particularly suitable. The stole pattern in this chapter uses fabric paints now readily available and

rich with new possibilities for vestment design. The design features doves descending into flames of fire.

The Sunday after Pentecost celebrates the doctrine of the Holy Trinity, a significant and mysterious understanding of God as three-in-one and one-in-three. The unity of the Trinity is commonly represented by three intertwined circles, a simple symbol that captures this incomprehensible concept. Before recent reforms in the Anglican church, ordinary time was designated the season of Trinity and many churches continue to clothe their sanctuary and ministers in raiments adorned with symbols of the Trinity rather than of Pentecost. The pieced chasuble in this chaper incorporates the intertwined circles symbolic of the Trinity with the traditional seven flames representative of Pentecost. A cotton chasuble helps to sustain the minister—layered in vestments during this season that spans the hot summer months of the Northern Hemisphere. Pieced cotton quilted to cotton lining with bound edges provides the body needed for a graceful-yet-cool chasuble.

The chasuble is constructed using the paper foundation method. This method allows for great freedom, while simultaneously providing accuracy and stability. The overall green design—with subtly intertwining rings, gold highlights, and seven intersecting flames created from red cloth—looks complicated, but detailed instructions are provided for each step. The preparation is a bit of work, but well worth the effort once you begin to sew. It may be helpful to copy one of the template illustrations and color it in with colored pencils for a visual color guide.

This book concludes with a small but essential vestment, the pocket or visitation stole, which is made reversible in white and purple. It is commonly carried in the minister's car or briefcase and is used for visitations and emergencies. A small bag (burse) is ideal to protect and house the stole and the companion pieces that make up the pastoral care kit: a small pyx for hosts and an oil stock.

FABRIC REQUIREMENTS

Stole (6" wide by 122" long, finished)

White silk or cotton, prepared for dyeing, if available: 1½ yards of 44" width.
Gold or red lining: 1½ yards of 44" width.
Non-fusible, light to midweight interfacing: 2 yards.
Chain or gold cording: 8"–10" length.
Sulky® iron-on transfer pen.
Synthrapol® prewash to prepare fabric for dyeing.
Silk paints: red, yellow, and blue.
Gutta or water-based paint resist and a small-nozzled dispenser.
Brushes, natural sponge, spray bottles.
Rubbing alcohol and cotton swabs.
Permanent fabric markers: optional.
Metallic or other ornamental threads: optional.
A large plastic sheet.

Chasuble (58" wide, 58" long in back, and 56" long in front, finished)

Green cotton base for the chasuble and lining: 5¼ yards of 44" width.
Gold cotton for the lining and chasuble piecing: 3¼ yards of 44" width.
Six additional shades of green cotton to coordinate with the base green—lights, darks, and mediums: 1 yard each.
Five to six reds, oranges, and a violet for the fire pieces: ½ yard each.
Postal wrapping paper or other 30" by 5 yard roll of paper.
White banner paper or other lightweight paper: two rolls (28" by 5 yards).
A yardstick compass.
Glue stick.
Clear template plastic: one sheet of 18" by 24", plus five sheets of 24" by 36" (plastic template or cardboard).
A quarter-inch-seam marking aid: optional.
Fine-grit sandpaper: one sheet.
Markers or crayons: red, green, and gold.

Pocket Stole (2" wide by 68" long, finished) and Burse (a 8" by 4" bag)

White and purple silk/synthetic satin or moiré: ¼ yard each of 44", or two yards each of white and purple 2" wide ribbon.
Sheer weight non-fusible interfacing: ¼ yard.
White and silver (or gold instead of white and silver) ribbon or braid: 1 yard of ⅜".
Narrow silver (or gold) cording: 4¼ yards.
Remnant of velvet or silver cloth: ¼ yard or a 9" square.
Velcro™: 8"

A PAINTED OVERLAY STOLE

Sizing

The stole is some 20" at its broadest point across the back and hangs 54" down the front. Adjust the stole length by altering pattern piece 2. Adjust the back cape by altering the outside curved edge of piece 1.

Prepare the Yardage

1. Prewash the cloth to remove any fabric finish. Avoid permanent press, water-repellent, or stain-repellent fabrics. If the fabric you purchased is not prepared for dyeing, use Synthrapol® to wash out sizing and impurities. Preshrink the fabric and lining in the dryer without dryer sheets. Press well.

2. Draft the stole pattern 11 following the general instructions on page 50. From the fabric, lining, and the interfacing, cut one of collar piece 1 on the grain and on the fold. Cut two of piece 2 from the fabric, lining and the interfacing. Add an extra ½" around the perimeter of both sections of the stole fabric. This excess will be trimmed after the stole is removed from the work surface.

3. Practice. Before beginning to paint, fix a remnant of the prepared fabric to the work surface and play with the resist and paints. A fine-tipped plastic dispenser for the resist facilitates a fine, even line. A clear resist used on white fabric will leave a white dove outline. Apply paint to the fabric with paintbrushes of varying size, sponges, or a spray bottle. Silk paint is water-soluble before it's fixed and handles similarly to watercolors on paper. It spreads into the fabric, leaving soft, blended edges that create an intermediary color—perfect for a fire image. Try working on dry and wet fabric samples until you are satisfied with the result. Dry fabric is more difficult to work on but allows for

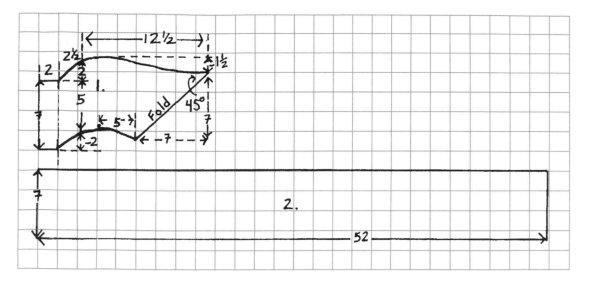

Pattern 11. Overlay stole in two sections, 1. collar (cut one on fold), and 2. tail (cut two).
Scale: one square = 2 inches.

strong color; wet fabric is easier to work on but dilutes the color. A combination of the two will give depth to the flames.

4. Cover the work surface with a clean plastic sheet and fix the fabric to the work surface with pins, staples, or masking tape-the fabric should be taut but not strained. Attach the fabric within the extra ½" allowance added in step 2. If space allows, butt the fabric where the seams will join for a flowing design across the seams.

5. Lightly sketch the design of flames and doves descending onto the fabric. If you are not confident about drawing your own design, have the chapter divider page with the illustrated stole enlarged at a copy shop. The illustration is to scale—1" equals 10". Following the manufacturer's instructions for the iron-on transfer pen, transfer the enlarged drawing onto the right side of the fabric. You may choose to delineate the dove's body by applying gutta to the body of the dove rather than the mere outline. Experiment and choose the method you find most pleasing.

6. Carefully paint the dove image outlines with the resist, by brush or with a small plastic, nozzled dispenser. Try to keep the outline contained and thin. Be sure that your lines are solid and that they penetrate the fabric completely. Allow to dry.

7. Pour a little paint into a small container or plate. Primary colors are recommended because from them you can mix all of the colors. You will need red, yellow, and mixtures (oranges) to make fire.

Remember, the colors will mix as they merge on the fabric. Add some blue to the red for violet shadows within the flames.

8. Apply the paint following the sketched design. You may want to achieve some definition of the flames by working an area, allowing it to dry, then coming back to work the adjoining area. Try to avoid over-flooding the gutta resist: it may break down and cause the paint to seep into the resist area. If you wish, use fabric salt on wet dye to create color explosions. Once the painting is dry, you may use rubbing alcohol applied with a cotton swab to create highlights, or markers for definition.

9. After the fabric is completely dry, iron it to fix the paints. Follow the manufacturer's directions.

10. Hand wash the fabric to remove the resist. Allow it to dry and then press.

11. If desired, embellish your design with machine or hand embroidery. A gold metallic thread especially befits the holy flames.

Complete the Stole

12. Trim off the ½" tacking allowance, using the pattern as a guide to re-cut the stole. Following the general instructions on page 48, apply the interfacing to both sections of the stole top.

13. Pin and stitch the stole collar (piece 1) in a ½" seam to the top edge of the stole tails (piece 2). Be sure to have the two tails on the correct sides of

the stole according to your painting and design. Check the overall length and trim the bottom edge if necessary.

14. Finish the stole following the general instructions on page 51.

15. Once the stole is completed, hold the stole in place by tacking the chain or ribbon at the dots found on the collar pattern (piece 1); or 5" in along the neck line from the center back fold.

A PAPER-PIECED CHASUBLE

Sizing

To adjust the chasuble's size, make your square—or rectangle, if need be—of paper. You may need to enlarge or reduce the ring size if you make extensive alterations. Place the rings and lines on the paper as directed, regardless of size changes.

Fabric Key

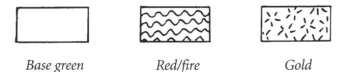

Base green   Red/fire   Gold

All the other drawn fabric patterns are the six variations of the green.

Draft the Pattern

This pattern is drafted a bit differently from the others. Draw the design onto a large sheet of paper and this will become your pattern. First make the templates, then the paper foundations from the drawn design. Stitch the fabric onto the paper foundations, piece it into sections, and then stitch it to the lining foundation. Refer to the pattern drawing as you follow the instructions. Use a pencil to draft the pattern because you will be asked to erase a few lines. If you are making a chasuble based on a square, you may opt to project Pattern 11 onto a sheet of paper taped to a wall until it is your desired size. Trace the pattern and skip to step 11.

1. On a large flat surface lay two 58" lengths of postal wrapping or other 30"-wide paper side by side. Tape the center where the edges of the two sheets of paper meet together. Tape the back side just enough to be secure; it will be removed later. Trim the paper to yield a 58" square with the seam dead center.

2. Tape together a 36" square without regard to where the seam falls. Use the yardstick compass to draw a 35" diameter circle and a 30" inner circle. Cut out the resultant 2½" wide ring to use for a circle template. Mark the ring into two halves.

3. Using the two half marks, center the ring on the seamed 58" square of paper. Place the bottom edge of the ring along the bottom edge of the paper and trace the ring onto the paper. The bottom edge of the ring is your hem line.

4. Two inches below the top edge—the edge opposite the hem length—mark a horizontal line across the paper's width. The area above the marked line is the extra length allowance for the chasuble back.

5. Place the ring template with one edge tangent (just touching) to the marked front shoulder line and one edge along the side edge of the paper square. Trace the ring onto the paper and do the same on the opposite side. You now have three intertwining circles drawn onto your square, exactly mirrored on the two paper halves.

6. To be sure both sides are identical, you may want to fold your paper in half along the seam for this next step. Draw a curve from the outside edge of the top circle where it is tangent to the paper edge to connect with the outside edge of the bottom circle. Follow the natural curve suggested by the outside edges of the circles. This will be the bottom edge of the chasuble. Cut the paper along this curve and open out flat (see Pattern 11).

7. Measure 4½" to the left of the center seam along the back and front shoulder lines and place a dot there. Draw a line from the 4½" dot on the back shoulder line to the intersecting point of the center paper seam and the 2" front shoulder line. This is the back neck line. Draw another line from the 4½" front dot to the ring intersection to make the front neck line. Repeat on the right side to create a V-back neckline. Do not draw a front neck line on the right side. You now have your base chasuble pattern (see illustration at the beginning of this chapter).

8. Set a straight edge at the center point of the base circle. Rotate the straight edge until it falls tangent to the far left edge of the right circle. Draw a line that reaches from the top edge of the base ring to the top edge of the paper and label it line "a." Do the same on the opposite side (see Pattern 11).

9. Rotate the straight edge until it spans from the same base center point to the tangent at the left of the upper left circle. Draw line "b" from the base point to the outside edge of the paper. Repeat on the right side.

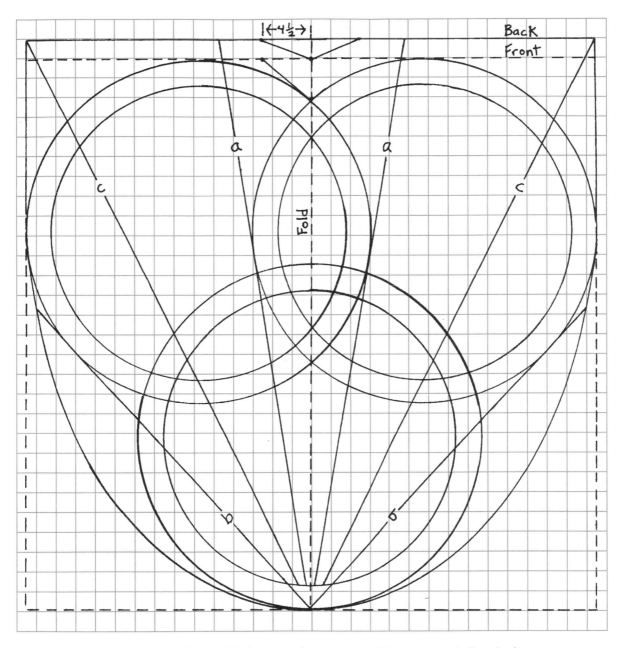

Pattern 11. Pieced chasuble from a 58" square—read instructions before drafting.
Scale: one square = 2 inches.

10. Rotate the straight edge once more until it spans from the base point to the upper corner of the paper. Draw the line from the inside edge of the base ring to the paper's corner and label the line "c." Repeat on the other side.

11. To simplify the piecing, erase the lines that create small, awkward areas. The lines to erase are circled and marked with an "x" on Figure 11-C11. When you make your front templates along the shoulder line (step 16) erase the marked lines encircled with a dash. The figure shows half of the pattern—remember to erase from both sides of the pattern. You now have your pattern drafted and are ready to make templates.

12. Separate the pattern along the center seam and cut away the inside of the V from the back neckline. Write "fold" along the center on one pattern half and set the other pattern half aside. Lines "b," "c," and "a" divide the pattern half into four sections. Assign each section a number (or color); then, on each internal section produced by the ring lines, assign the numbers given in Figure

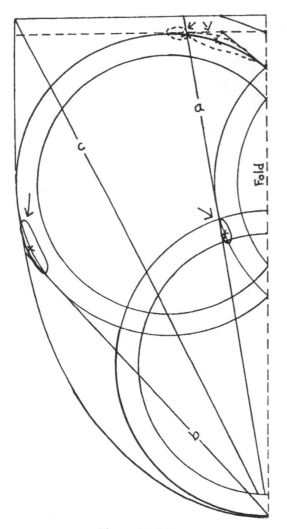

Figure 11-C11.
Erase encircled lines to simplify piecing.

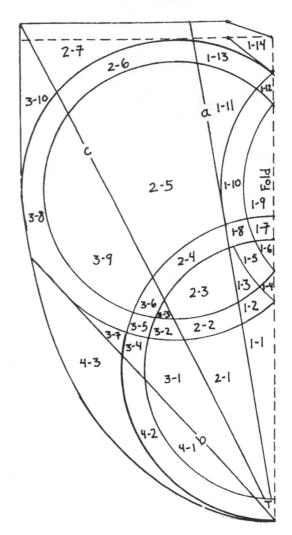

Figure 11-C12.
The master template, numbered by section and piece.

11-C12. Do not assign a separate number to the areas above the front shoulder and neck lines. Mark the base triangle "T." This is your master template. Set it aside.

13. Mirror your numbers on the other pattern half. Be careful that every section has the same numbers assigned on the master template. On each section that borders the center, mark with three dots ∴ to remind yourself to place them on a fold. When transcribing the numbers on the mirrored half, place all the numbers right side up and toward the chasuble center (see Figure 11-C14). This will help you to know the placement of each piece. As you work, if you question which way a piece goes, remember the numbers are upright and toward the chasuble center.

14. Scribble red with a marker or colored pencil along lines "b," "c," "a," and the center fold lines so that the red extends slightly into all of the sections that

border each line. Do not scribble red along the lines inside the rings except where the line runs tangent to the ring along 3-8. The red scribbles will indicate where to place the fire fabrics. Mark with gold all of the ring intersection pieces (1-4, 1-8, 1-12, 3-5) and the 'T' triangle. With a green marker, mark a directional line on each piece to help you know which way to place the fabric on the foundation pieces (Figure 11-C14).

15. Carefully cut out all of the numbered sections, leaving the master template whole. Do not cut on the front shoulder line—erase it. Label pieces 1-13, 1-14, 2-6, 2-7 and 3-10 with a "B" for back. Glue all the pattern sections to a piece of template plastic or cardboard that is at least ¼" larger than the perimeter of each piece. Add a ¼" seam allowance around each section except the edges marked for placement on a fold. On the pieces that have a long tail-like extension, measure ¼"

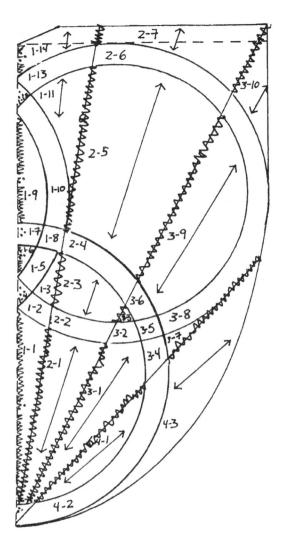

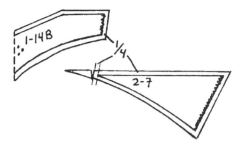

Figure 11-C15. Add ¼" around each piece before cutting plastic template, the fold line excepted. Cut off the tail ¼" beyond pointed line confluences.

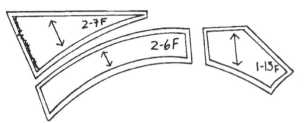

Figure 11-C16. The front-shoulder templates.

Figure 11-C14. To indicate the flame areas, scribble red over lines a, b, c, and the center fold outside of the rings. Be sure all numbers are upright and toward the centers. Mark direction lines for fabric placement in the background areas.

beyond the pointed end of the section and cut off the excess seam allowance beyond this ¼" measure (Figure 11-C15). Cut out the templates exactly on the seam allowance line.

16. Make the front neck and shoulder templates. On the master template, lay a piece of clear plastic template over piece 3-10 and trace it, stopping at the front shoulder line. Label the template 3-10F (front), add a ¼" seam allowance, the red scribbles, the directional lines, and cut it out. Lay clear plastic template over pieces 1-13 and 1-14. Trace a front 1-13 by eliminating the dashed encircled line (see Figure 11-C11) and replacing it with the front neck and shoulder lines (Figure 11-C16). Label it 1-13F, add a ¼" seam allowance, and cut it out (1-14 is used for the chasuble back only). Lay

another piece of clear template over pieces 2-6 and 2-7. Eliminate the dashed encircled line and use the front shoulder line to trace templates 2-6F and 2-7F. You will need to trace one and then the other so that you can move the plastic to accommodate the ¼" seam allowances along the shared line. Transfer the red scribbles to 2-7 and transcribe the number onto 2-6F with care (upright and toward the chasuble center), as this is a tricky template to piece once it is cut out. Cut both templates out.

17. Make the paper foundation templates. Set the fold templates aside. Trace the remaining templates onto white banner paper. As you work, transfer the numbers to the back side of each piece, being careful that all the numbers are upright and toward the chasuble centers. Mark the directional lines, red edges, and gold areas where applicable, on the top side of each paper foundation. Trace four of each piece (two right side up and two wrong side up for the mirror side) except the T, B, and F templates. Trace two of them (one right side up, one wrong side up).

18. To make the fold foundation pieces, draw a light line down a length of paper wide enough to accommodate the full width of the templates. Once unfolded, most are around 8" wide. Template 1-14B is 18½" wide and needs only one foundation. Twice for the rest of the fold templates, align the fold edge along the drawn line and trace the outside edges of the template, then flip the template

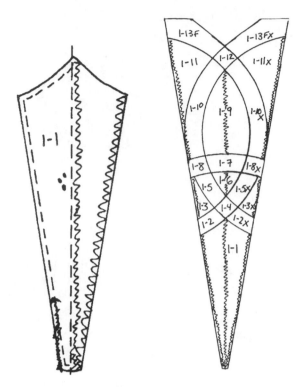

Figure 11-C18. Make a
full width template from
the pieces on the fold line.

Figure 11-C19. Attach an
"x" to one of the duplicate
pieces in the center sec-
tions, front and back.

over—maintaining the center alignment—and
trace again (Figure 11-C18). You now have full-
size center-piece foundations. Label. Add red to
1-1, 1-6, 1-9, and gold to T, 1-4, and 1-2. Cut out
all of the traced paper foundations.

19. Gather all the section 1 (center) paper foundations. Lay them out in order to make the center
front and back panels. Remember that you have
added a seam allowance and will have some overlap. Use the master template to help. To make the
piecing easier, attach an "x" to the right side (as
you face them) of foundations numbered: 1-2,
1-3, 1-5, 1-8, 1-10, 1-11, 1-13F and 1-13B (Figure
11-C19).

20. Make one more plastic or cardboard template,
3½" high with a 2⅛" base leg and 2½" top leg
(Figure 11-C20). Since it will be used on fabric,
you may want to glue fine-grit sand paper to the
back of the template. Label the template "R" for
ring. This template will be used to cut the greens
for piecing over the ring foundations. Now you
are set up and ready to work with fabric!

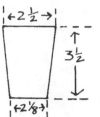

Figure 11-C20. Make a trapezoidal template
3½" high for filling the rings.

Prepare the Lining and Binding

21. Cut 118" lengths from the base green and gold lining fabrics. Trim the green length to 25" wide and
the gold into two 19" widths. With right sides
together, stitch one gold length to the green length
using a ½" seam. Stitch the other gold length to
the remaining long green edge to yield a 61" by
118" lining unit. Press the seams open. Lay the

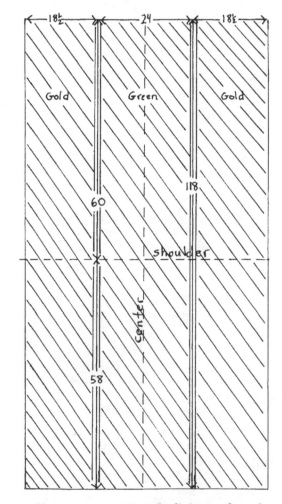

Figure 11-C21. Piece the lining and mark
the shoulder and center lines.

lining on a large flat surface, wrong side up. Measure 60" up from one end and draw the shoulder line across the width of the lining at the 60" mark (Figure 11-C21). Mark the center line of the lining along the entire length. Set the lining aside.

22. Cut two 28" by 2" strips from the green base fabric and two 4" by 2" red pieces. Stitch the red pieces to one end of each green strip in a ¼" seam. Along one long end on each strip, press under ½". Be sure the two strips are opposites. Set aside. These strips will be used to cover the shoulder seams on the chasuble top.

23. Following the general instructions on page 48 and using the base green fabric, cut a 36" by 2½" bias strip to finish the neck edge; cut and join a bias strip 7½ yards by 2½". A 36" on-grain square of fabric is sufficient. Set the bias strips aside and use the remaining fabric and lining remnants for the chasuble top.

24. Trace and cut forty-six R pieces from each of the seven different green cottons (the base plus six); and about thirty-eight pieces, 5" high and tapered, from the variety of fire colors. Sections 1-13F, 2-6F, and 3-8 are oversized rings and require some green swatches cut 5" high instead of the standard 3½" height of template R.

25. Fill in the ring foundations. Gather all the ring foundation pieces except the seven gold ones. The goal is to fill in the paper foundation ring segments with the variety of green R pieces. As you add the R pieces to the ring foundations, alternate the hues. When adding red into rings 1-10 and 3-8, mix in the red patches with the R patches—perhaps two or three reds to one R. For interest, you may, on rare occasion, want to add in a "zip of fire" as you fill the rings.

26. Place the first R piece of fabric right side up along one narrow edge of a ring foundation. Allow the

---

Hints for Foundation Piecing (a paper-backed method of piecing)

- The key to foundation piecing is to use oversized swatches of fabric when you fill the foundations. Always make sure that the fabric swatch exceeds the outside edge of the paper foundation, then trim it to size after stitching it to the foundation and pressing it open.

- For the best results, taper all of the fabric strips in the same manner you cut the template in step 20. A good rule of thumb is to taper the strips so they are ⅛" to ¼" narrower along the bottom width than on the top width.

- For an organic appearance, be free with color; let chance play a large part in how it's arranged; for a more formal design, follow an orderly plan and piece all like-numbered sections in the exact same way—remember to mirror your work.

- Work all of the pieces of one section at a time. Repeat what you do on one piece for the other pieces with the same number. This repetition will give the chasuble a balanced and unified overall design. Remember that half the pieces mirror the other half.

- Try to avoid a piecing seam near the foundation edges. Insert a narrow piece before a wider one to adjust the fabric width needed to reach an edge. Think ahead and watch your fabric widths.

- When you piece the center front and back foundations, begin with the center fire fabrics and work out toward the edges. This method will help you to avoid having seams fall on the center lines.

- Do not put fire fabrics in T, 1-4, 1-7, or 1-12.

- Use a larger machine needle, size 14, to make it easier to remove the foundation later. In order to better secure the seam when you remove the foundation, use a smaller stitch length (18–20 stitches per inch).

- Press the units with a dry iron because the steam may distort the paper foundation.

- Stitch your fabric to the wrong, non-labeled, but sometimes colored side of the foundation so that you do not cover up your section numbers.

- Do not remove the paper foundations until you are ready to assemble the chasuble.

- The chasuble pattern consists of two basic parts: the rings themselves, referred to as the "ring foundations," and the background sections between and around the rings.

- For variety, you may want to cover a foundation with a single fabric, particularly the smaller and red sections 1-3, 3-7, and 4-1. To simplify the overall design, you may elect to cover all the background sections with a single color. Templates covered completely with a single color do not need paper foundations. Use your template as a pattern to cut the exact fabric shapes for each solid section.

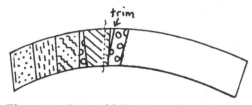

Figure 11-C26. Add the R template pieces to fill the ring foundations. Adjust the ring taper with the top fabric and trim excess along the seam allowance from the bottom fabric.

fabric to overlap the top and bottom paper edges. After the fabric is stitched on, trim the fabric to match the foundation. The fabric should always exceed the foundation height edges and then be trimmed to size after it's applied. With right sides together, position a second R piece on top of the first and stitch through all the layers using a ¼" seam. Press the second R piece open and add a third R piece to the second in the same manner. As you work, you may need to adjust the tapering to neatly fit the foundation pieces. Adjust it by placing the fabric swatch to be added exactly along the desired slant, and use this top fabric as your ¼" seam guide. Trim the fabric underneath to match the top fabric after you stitch it (Figure 11-C26). Continue adding R pieces until the foundation is covered. Baste the two end fabric patches to the foundation. Be sure the fabric patches are trimmed exactly along the foundation edges. Once completed, you should have a ring section covered with a variety of green fabrics contoured to the foundation.

27. Cut some 3½" strips from the gold fabrics and use them to cover the gold foundations as directed in step 26.

28. Gather the remaining foundation pieces. Cut strips from the variety of green fabrics and fire fabrics to exceed the height of the foundations—this size will vary according to the piece. Taper the strips (see hints above) and vary their widths for interest (Figure 11-C28). Cover all the foundation pieces with the green strips as directed in step 26. Place the strips vertically by following the green directional lines added in step 14, adjusting the slant of the fabric as necessary. Place fire colors where the foundations are scribbled red. Vary the width and number of fire fabrics to give an organic feel to the flames.

29. Lay out the master template to guide the filling and placement of the pieces. On a large smooth area, lay out the fabric-covered foundations as

you complete them. You should fill two sets, the front and back, half of which mimics and half of which mirrors the master template. Be careful that front pieces are together with front pieces and back pieces are together with back pieces. Use the completed foundations to inspire yourself to fill the remaining pieces until all the pieces are filled and placed in accordance with the master template. The design should be an overall green with subtle intertwining rings, gold highlights, and seven intersecting flames.

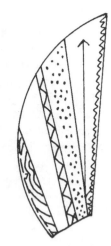

Figure 11-C28. Add vertical strips to fill the remaining templates.

Piecing the Chasuble

30. Steps 32 through 35 list the order in which the pieces are joined. First, review the following general instructions:

- Work systematically so that you don't lose track of where the piece goes when the foundation label is removed.
- To prepare a seam for stitching, lay two adjoining edges right sides together (see Figure 11-C31b) and check how the seams line up. Identify the key matching points (ends and intersecting ring seams but not necessarily the filling strips) and pin them first. Then pin the rest of the seam.
- All seams are ¼". After pinning but before stitching, check to see how the intersecting seams line up. The ring seams should all be in line. Adjust if necessary before stitching. Baste. It helps.
- After basting, check the basted pieces against the master template to assure accuracy.
- Do not backstitch at the beginning and end of the seams in case you need to rip out and re-stitch a seam. Ripping is as much a part of sewing as stitching.
- Use a size 11 or 12 machine needle and a stitch length of about 12–14 stitches per inch.
- Use a ¼" presser foot or walking foot with a ¼" guide.
- Press the seams closed to relax the stitching, then press in one direction. To help the intersecting seams line up accurately and to reduce the overall

bulk, press seams that will be joined in opposite directions before you stitch them. Doing so will give a smooth finish to the chasuble.

How to stitch curved seams:

31. Once the pieces to be joined are trimmed exactly along the paper foundation edges, remove the paper foundation. With the concave curve on top (Figure 11-C31a) match and pin the seam line by gently stretching the concave edge to fit the convex edge. Pin the key intersecting seams first (Figure 11-C31b). Hand baste in place. With the concave curve on top, stitch along the ¼" seam line, gently stretching the concave curve to fit the convex curve. Take care to keep the bottom side smooth by using your finger to smooth the fabric as it feeds into the machine. The small amount of pressure used to stretch the concave curve to fit the convex curve should keep a check on bothersome tucks. Press closed with the convex side up, then press toward the concave curve.

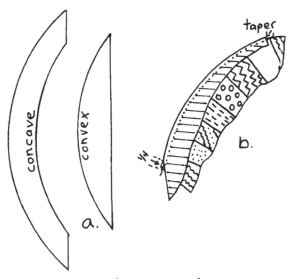

Figure 11-C31 a. The concave and convex curves. b. With convex curve on top, gently stretch the top fabric to fit the concave curve. Match the ends at the ¼" seam line and taper the tails ¼" off the edge.

32. Piece section 4. Stitch 4-1 to 4-2, then 4-2 to 4-3. Repeat for all four segments.
33. Piece section 2. Stitch 2-1 to 2-2 and 2-3 to 2-4, then 2-2 to 2-3. Stitch 2-5 to 2-6, then 2-6 to 2-7 (keep track of fronts and backs). Now join 2-4 to 2-5. Repeat for all four segments.
34. Piece section 3. Stitch 3-1 to 3-2, then 3-2 to 3-3. Stitch 3-4 to 3-5, then 3-5 to 3-6. Stitch the top

edge of the joined 3-1 section to the bottom edge of the joined 3-4 section. Take care to match the intersecting seams. Stitch 3-9 to 3-8, then 3-8 to 3-7—line up the bottom ends to get the placement right. Stitch the joined 3-8 section to the joined 3-4 section. Finish by adding 3-10 along the top. Be sure to maintain the straight line "c" and keep track of the fronts and backs. Repeat for all four segments.

35. Now you are ready to join the two section 1 segments. Join 1-1 to 1-2, then add 1-3. Stitch 1-2x to 1-4, then add 1-5. Stitch the joined 1-1 unit to the 1-4 unit. Now join 1-3x to 1-5x, then add 1-6 and stitch the unit to the joined 1-1 and 1-4 unit. Let's call this "D" for done. Stitch 1-8 to 1-7, then add 1-8x and stitch the unit to D (which we will continue to call D). Stitch 1-9 to 1-10, then add 1-11. Stitch 1-10x to 1-12, then add 1-13—again, keep track of the fronts and backs. Stop the stitching ¼" shy of the neck edge where 1-13F joins to 1-12. Fold back the unseamed ¼" of 1-13F and, when the time comes, pin 1-13Fx to the freed ¼" seam allowance of 1-12 to create the V neckline (Figure 11-C35). Stitch the joined 1-9 unit to the 1-12 unit. Stitch 1-11x to 1-13x. Add 1-14 to the back unit. Join the 1-9 and 1-12 unit to the 1-11x unit being careful to maintain the front and back. Now join this unit to D. Remove any paper foundation that may remain on any of the joined sections.

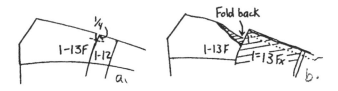

Figure 11-C35. a. Stop the stitching ¼" shy of the neck edge where 1-13F joins to 1-12; b. fold back the unseamed ¼" of 1-13F and stitch 1-13Fx to the freed ¼" seam allowance of 1-12 to create the front V neckline.

Join the Units to the Lining

36. The chasuble top sections will be joined as they are added to the lining. This is a "sew and flip" or quilt-as-you-go method. Use a walking foot on your machine to produce smooth, even seams. Smooth the prepared lining on a large flat surface. With wrong sides together, lay the front section 1 on the lining with the top edges of 1-13 aligned to the shoulder line (drawn on the lining). Place the

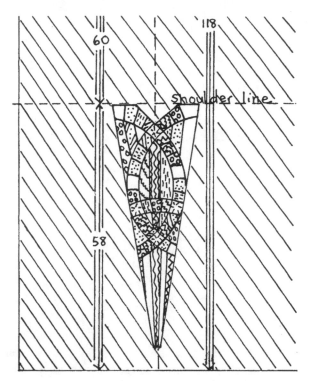

Figure 11-C36. Wrong sides together, place the front section 1 along the marked shoulder and center lines on the lining.

front on the 58" length of lining (Figure 11-C36). Be sure the center of section 1 is in perfect alignment with the center of the lining. Baste it in place.

37. With right sides together, lay one front section 2 along the section 1 seam line (line "a"). Check to be sure that the intersecting ring seams line up. Pin, baste, and stitch in a ¼" seam. Press the seam closed to relax the stitching, then press section 2 open. Baste in position along line "c." Repeat on the reciprocal front side.

38. With right sides together, lay one front section 3 along the section 2 seam line (line "c"). Check to be sure that the intersecting ring seams line up. Pin, baste, and stitch in a ¼" seam. Press the seam closed to relax the stitching, then press section 3 open. Baste in position along line "b." Repeat on the reciprocal front side.

39. With right sides together, stitch patch T along the base of the joined sections 1, 2, and 3. Press down and baste in place.

40. With right sides together, lay one front section 4 along the section 3 seam line (line "b"). Check to be sure that the intersecting ring seams line up. Pin, baste, and stitch in a ¼" seam. Press the seam closed to relax the stitching, then press section 4

open and baste in place. Repeat on the reciprocal front side. Trim the lining along the outside edge of the chasuble front.

41. Smooth the lining on a large flat surface. With wrong sides together, lay the back section 1 on the lining with the top edges of 1-14 aligned to the shoulder line drawn on the lining and butted along the top edges of the front 1-13 sections. Place the back on the 60" length of lining. Be sure the center of section 1 is in perfect alignment with the center of the lining. Baste it in place. Repeat steps 37 to 40 to complete the back, substituting the back sections for the front sections.

42. Retrieve the 2" strips prepared in step 22. These will be used on the outside to conceal the butted raw edges of the chasuble along the shoulder lines. Right sides together, lay the unturned long edge of one of the prepared 2" strips along the edge of the front at the shoulder line (Figure 11-C42). Place the seam between the red and the green on the strip toward the outside edge, where it complements the red on chasuble front and back (the strip is oversized so that you have adjustment room). Pin and trim the excess length from the strip at the outside edge and neckline. Stitch in place using a ½" seam. Repeat on the other side. Press the strip to conceal the butted chasuble shoulder edges and pin the folded edge along the chasuble back. Blind stitch it in place.

43. Smooth the chasuble on a large flat surface and attach the lining to it with safety pins. Turn the chasuble over and check to be sure that the lining is pinned smoothly and without tucks. By hand or with a machine walking foot, quilt the chasuble front and back by stitching in the ditch (seam) of the inner and outer ring outlines. The quilt-as-you-go and ring contour stitching is sufficient quilting. If desired, add more quilting to the chasuble. Remove the pins when all the quilting is completed.

Finishing the Chasuble

44. Using the master template and the chasuble neck edges, cut open the lining neck edge. Stay stitch the neck edge through both thicknesses. Using the neck binding prepared in step 23, bind the neck edge following the general instructions on page 48. To bind the inside V corners, clip the inside corner of each V to the stay-stitching. When

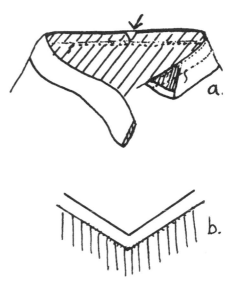

Figure 11-C44. a. Pull the corner straight at the clip to attach the binding; b. fold the binding to the inside and stitch in place.

A POCKET STOLE AND BURSE

A pocket stole is a small stole used for visitations. Instead of crosses, three horizontal rows of braid along the bottom of the stole ends may be applied. Be sure the spacing between each row of braid and from the bottom of the stole's edges are identical on both sides.

1. Draft the pattern on page 138 and cut two lengths from the white and purple fabrics and from the interfacing.
2. Attach the interfacing to the wrong side of the white fabric following the general instructions on page 48.
3. Stitch the center back neck seams in a ½" seam. Press seams open.

Adorn the Fabrics

4. Normally, both sides of a visitation stole are adorned with simple ribbon crosses placed at each end and at the center. Cut the ribbon into twelve 3" sections. Turn under both ends of two cut ribbon sections and one end of four ½" sections. Trim the folded ends to ¼".
5. Center the ribbons with one end turned under lengthwise at the four stole ends, having the unturned end flush with the cut stole end (Figure 11-PS5a). Whip stitch in place. Overlay four

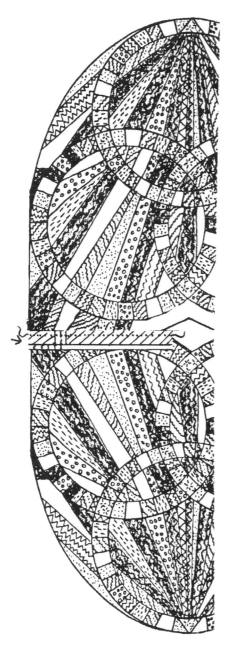

Figure 11-C42. Attach strip prepared in step 22 at the shoulder to enclose the seam.

attaching the binding to the chasuble, keep the binding straight at the inside V corners by pulling the corners straight as you stitch (Figure 11-C44a). Since the binding is narrow and on the bias, you need not mitre the binding. Simply fold the binding over and blind stitch it in place (Figure 11-C44b).

45. Use the hem binding prepared in step 23 to bind the hem edge, following the general instructions on page 48.

Bibliography

Appostolos-Cappadona, Diane. *Dictionary of Christian Art.* New York: Continuum, 1994.

Armstrong, Regis J., O.F.M., and Ignatius C. Brady, O.F.M., eds. *Francis and Clare, The Complete Works.* The Classics of Western Spirituality. New York: Paulist Press, 1982.

Brauer, Jerald C., ed. *The Westminster Dictionary of Church History.* Philadelphia: Westminster Press, 1971.

Cirlot, J. E. *A Dictionary of Symbols.* New York: Philosophical Library, 1971.

Collins, Harold E. *The Church Edifice and Its Appointments.* Philadelphia: Dolphin Press, 1940.

Complete Guide to Sewing. New York: Reader's Digest Association, 1976.

Complete Guide to Needlework. New York: Reader's Digest Association, 1979.

Contini, Mila. *Fashion from Ancient Egypt to the Present Day.* New York: Crescent Books, 1965.

Cross, F. L, ed. *The Oxford Dictionary of the Christian Church.* 2d ed. New York: Oxford University Press, 1974.

Dearmer, Percy, Rev. *The Ornaments of the Ministers.* London: A. R. Mowbray, 1920.

Dolby, Anastasia. *Church Vestments: Their Origin, Use and Ornament.* London: Chapman and Hall, 1868.

Episcopal Church, The. The Book of Common Prayer. New York: Seabury Press, 1979.

———. *Lesser Feasts and Fasts 2000.* New York: Church Publishing Corporation, 2001.

Gent, Barbara, and Betty Sturges. *The New Altar Guild Book.* Harrisburg, Pa.: Morehouse Publishing, 1996.

Hansen, Henny Harald. *Costumes and Styles.* New York: E. P. Dutton, 1956.

Hargrave, Harriet. *From Fiber to Fabric.* Lafayette, Calif.: C & T Publishing, 1997.

Hatchett, Marion J. *Commentary on the American Prayer Book.* New York: Seabury Press, 1981.

———. *A Manual of Ceremonial for the New Prayer Book.* Sewanee, Tenn.: School of Theology, University of the South, 1977.

Hines, Dick. *Dressing for Worship, A Fresh Look at What Christians Wear in Church.* Cambridge, England: Grove Books Ltd., 1996.

Legg, J. Wickham. *Church Ornaments and Their Civil Antecedents.* Cambridge, England: University Press, 1917.

Lesage, Robert. *Vestments and Church Furniture.* Translated by Fergus Murphy. New York: Hawthorn Books, 1960.

Liberal Catholic Church, The. *A Manual for the Making of Vestments Used in the Liberal Catholic Church.* Needlecraft Series. New York: St. Alban's Press, n.d.

Mackrille, Lucy Vaughan Hayden. *Church Embroidery and Church Vestments.* Chevy Chase, Md.: Cathedral Studios, 1939.

Mayer-Thurman, Christie C. *Raiment for the Lord's Service: A Thousand Years of Western Vestments.* Chicago: Art Institute, 1975.

McCloud, Henry J. *Clerical Dress and Insignia of the Roman Catholic Church.* Milwaukee: Bruce Publishing Co., 1948.

Megivern, James J. *Worship and Liturgy.* Wilmington, N.C.: Consortium Books, 1978.

Metford, J. C .J. *The Dictionary of Christian Lore and Legend.* London: Thames and Hudson, 1983.

Norris, Herbert. *Church Vestments, Their Origin and Development.* London: J. M. Dent and Sons, Ltd., 1949.

O'Connell, J. *The Celebration of the Mass: A Study of the Rubrics of the Roman Missal.* Milwaukee: Bruce Publishing Co., 1940.

Pahl, Ellen, ed. *The Quilter's Ultimate Visual Guide From A-Z.* Emmaus, Pa.: Rodale Press, 1997.

Perry, Patricia, ed. *The Vogue Sewing Book.* New York: Vogue Patterns, 1970.

Piepkorn, Arthur Carl. *The Survival of the Historic Vestments in the Lutheran Church after 1555*. Saint Louis: Concordia Seminary Graduate Studies, 1958.

Post, W. Ellwood. *Saints, Signs and Symbols*. Harrisburg, Pa.: Morehouse Publishing, 1974.

Roulin, Dom E. A., O.S.B. *Vestments and Vesture: A Manual of Liturgical Art*. Translated by Dom Justin McCann, O.S.B. Westminster, Md.: Newman Press, 1950.

Russel, Douglas A. *Costume History and Style*. Englewood Cliffs, N.J.: Prentice-Hall, 1983.

Tyack, George S. *Historic Dress of the Clergy*. London: William Andrews & Co., 1897.

Weston, Lilla B. N. *Vestments and How to Make Them*. London: A. R. Mowbray, 1914.

Wilby, Noel MacDonald, and Elizabeth Carr. *How to Make Vestments*. London: Burns, Oates & Washbourne, Ltd., 1936.

Index of Patterns

⌒